Abbandonata
A WIFE DENIED

FRANCESCA FALLETTA MARCECA

Copyright © 2025 by Francesca Falletta Marceca

All rights reserved.

No part of this book may be reproduced in any form or by any electronic or mechanical means, including information storage and retrieval systems, without written permission from the author, except for the use of brief quotations in a book review.

Editing, Cover Design, and Interior Design: Jason Morgan at Plotworks Publishing

ISBN (print): 978-1-960936-59-2

To my son, the inspiration behind this book. Though it was written during a challenging time, a flower blossomed from the rubble. I needed to escape from bad thoughts, so I picked up a pen and started to write. I noticed the more I was writing, the calmer I was.

Also, a heartfelt thank you to my family for your unwavering support, encouragement, and pride. Some of you helped with editing, some took time from their daily busy schedule, and others cheered me and inspired me to keep writing. Most of all, your constant love and pride kept me going.

I hope this story will inspire anyone who's going through a difficult time to write or pick up a hobby you enjoy, so your mind can be free of worries.

Chapter One

Why, years ago, were women subjected to cruelty and a lack of respect, with nothing being done about it? I'm talking about marriages without love.

In the early 1900s in the towns of Sicily, if a young man wanted a young woman to be his wife, regardless of wealth or reason, he would fight for her. He would gather a team of young men and they would physically take the girl. She might resist, but in the end, she would lose due to the strength and force of the gang of young men.

Today, we call this abduction.

The young woman would be taken to a secret hideaway where the doors were closed, locked, and bolted. Her soon-to-be husband would be in there with her. It was understood that once this capture was successful there was no return. This was referred to as an elopement by force, and the law did nothing about it as long as he made her his wife. They would be left there until the marriage was consummated, only then being allowed to come out and live as husband and wife. She had no choice but to live in a loveless marriage.

Years later, it still happened, but with less force than the brutal kidnappings of the past. Instead, they transformed into tricks and schemes, calculated to achieve success. Often, these were orchestrated by jilted boyfriends who couldn't accept being rejected.

The boyfriend would inform his ex-girlfriend that young men were coming to abduct her much younger sister and force her into an elopement. But it was a lie, designed to divert attention and protection away from the ex-girlfriend, who was the real target.

With all eyes focused on the younger sister, the ex-girlfriend had little or no protection, making it much easier to abduct her. Though she fought tooth and nail, she lost, and there was no returning home; otherwise, she would live a life as a so-called spinster, with no prospect of marriage. In those times, love or being loved was not always an option for a young woman.

It still went on up until the 1980s, when it became a more modern form of elopement. A couple attracted to each other, would indulge in a relationship – the young man, thirsty for sex, would woo the girl with sweetness and convince her to sleep with him. If she found herself with child, they would agree to run away together because she was too scared to tell her parents about the pregnancy. They would stay away for three weeks or two days, depending on his financial means. It was an easy way for underage boys and girls to sleep together, as even though premarital sex was not approved, it was accepted once they had eloped.

Running away was pretty much accepted and happened often. People would say, *They love each other, and he's going to marry her,* or *He'll make a decent woman of her yet.* Her decency—not his—was always their top priority.

There were some parents who were outraged, perhaps because of his family background, financial status, or lack of education, or maybe just plain embarrassment. Whatever the reason, they would stand firm, ignoring their daughter and her new husband for some time. But eventually they too would give in and forgive.

Some parents thanked God they now had one less mouth to feed. Others encouraged their daughter to run away with the boy, especially if he came from a wealthy family. Soon after their return and the forgiveness from the parents, the young woman's parents would prepare a Catholic wedding so she didn't live in shame or give birth out of wedlock.

The couple would live happily ever after for about seven months.

Then he'd realize that they'd been too young to get married, that they were living in a loveless marriage, that he was trapped.

This is what happened to Nina.

Chapter Two

Nina was not the brightest nor prettiest girl in her small town, but she had a good-natured soul.

She lived in Bagheria, near Palermo. Life there was vastly different from what was known in the U.S., though she didn't comprehend the difference, as she was content with her family, friends, and familiar way of life. At fifteen years old, Nina first laid eyes on a young man to whom she was instantly attracted.

The object of her affection was Nicola Niceli, a seventeen-year-old Sicilian. He had very little money in his pockets, which discouraged him from socializing or pursuing girls. He worked with his father, doing cement work on Nina's uncle's property.

When Nicola first saw Nina, there was an undeniable spark, albeit mostly on her part.

Nina fell head over heels at first sight.

There was little communication between them, but the more she saw him, the more her heart fluttered. At her uncle's house, she would hide and stare longingly at Nicola from behind wooden shutters. She admired the sweat trickling down his forehead and bare shoulders, evidence of his strength and diligence under Sicily's scorching summer heat.

One particularly sweltering day, Nina remarked to her aunt, "How could those workers accomplish anything when it's so hot?"

Her aunt then suggested making a pitcher of iced water and instructed Nina, "Get glasses and bring it out to them."

This was music to Nina's eager ears, as she wouldn't dare propose it herself. She prepared four glasses on a tray with the iced pitcher, fixed her ponytail, pinched her cheeks, and headed outside.

As she crossed the patio's threshold, she saw him kneeling, mixing wet cement. He looked up.

Their eyes locked, and she nearly dropped the tray. Flustered, she approached the other workers first, desperate to appear nonchalant about favoring him with refreshment.

After serving them, she turned to Nicola. His piercing grin intensified her nerves until the tray shook, spilling water.

He chuckled, aware of her nervousness.

"Would you like some water?" Nina offered in a soft voice.

"What else is on the menu?" he replied.

"I have cold water with ice, but you can have it warm if you'd prefer."

He stared, impressed by her wit. He knew he'd deserved the retort.

Over the following days, as he continued working the job for his father, Nina contrived reasons to linger.

Nicola saw through her excuses and showered her with compliments. He had only one goal in mind.

* * *

Nina's poor aunt suffered from excruciating arthritis pain in both knees. One day, her mother implored her, "Please Nina, can you go there and give your aunt a hand? Those workers are still there, and she needs you."

Not wanting to reveal her eagerness, Nina feigned disinterest. "Oh mom, do I have to? It's so boring there."

"Well, someone has to go," her mother said. "Would you rather stay home and watch your baby sister so I can go?"

Nina didn't want to risk losing her opportunity.

"No Mom," she said quickly, "I know how much you hate leaving the baby. I'll go."

Nina hurried to her aunt's house.

Upon arriving, she noticed the red truck belonging to Nicola's father was absent. Disappointed and saddened, she made her way to her aunt's bedroom.

Her aunt had taken a heavy dose of painkillers for her arthritis and told Nina she would like to sleep as the pills made her drowsy. The uncle was still at work and should be home later.

With her aunt in no shape to prepare dinner, Nina took it upon herself to cook for her.

In the kitchen, she turned on the radio and began cleaning vegetables. As she rinsed escarole by the sink, she thought she heard a truck on the property. She pushed aside the curtains over the sink, but saw no one, not a vehicle nearby. She continued rinsing the leafy vegetable with the water running and the radio on, all other noises muted in the kitchen.

Suddenly, a strong hand grabbed her shoulder. Then, another gripped her upper arm so tightly that she almost felt pain.

Nicola turned her to face him.

Again, they made eye contact. But this time it was more intense. Nina was now only inches from his face, feeling weak and helpless. He continued staring, his smile scaring her.

Silently, she asked herself, *What's he going to do?*

In that moment, the rest of the world faded away. He released her arms only to cup her face in his hands. She looked so angelic and helpless. Without any worry or concern for who might walk in, he pulled her face closer and planted his full lips on her mouth, kissing her passionately.

It was electrifying.

Nina's secret crush was focused on her too. She hoped it might lead to something special.

Soon, Nicola was giving her all the attention she'd craved from him.

* * *

In Bagheria, it was unacceptable for a teenage girl to be in the company of a young man alone unless he was family. So, in order to meet with Nicola, Nina would sneak out of her home. The secrecy thrilled her.

They'd meet at a discreet location, then walk to an abandoned farmhouse to spend time alone. A month later, Nina missed her period.

She was pregnant.

There would be no celebration. This was not news her parents would welcome. In their minds, a girl stayed pure until she married. Telling her family about the pregnancy was Nina's worst nightmare.

There was only one solution to this problem: run away with Nicola.

If they eloped, her pregnancy would be acceptable. Her parents could prepare for a Catholic wedding when she returned. This way, no one could say that their little girl was living in sin, or worse, accuse her of having a baby out of wedlock.

Seven months after their wedding, Nina and Nicola had their first child, a little girl they named Diana.

Then, cracks began to form in their happily ever after.

Nicola felt increasing pressure, felt as though he'd been trapped in a loveless marriage. It bristled beneath the surface of their relationship.

Yet, he continued providing for his family. He fathered another daughter with Nina. Over the years, Nina imagined maturity had helped him settle into their marriage.

For herself, Nina had no complaints. She was married. Her husband made good money as a contractor. They had two beautiful little girls and lived near her family in the hometown she was accustomed to. What more could Nina want?

Nicola traveled frequently. He claimed it was work taking him away from home.

Eventually, the gossip reached Nina—her husband was a womanizer, always chasing women around town. Some even witnessed him keeping company with much younger ladies.

Poor Nina preferred to deny the rumors. It was easier than accepting them and their consequences.

On rare occasions, she'd summon the nerve to confront her husband.

"I'm not saying it's true," Nina said gently, afraid to upset him. "But people in town are talking."

"Who do you believe?" Nicola defended himself. "Your husband or nasty gossip?"

Nina didn't answer. She never did, preferring to avoid a fight. Deep down, however, she knew there was truth to the rumors.

In a small town like Bagheria in rural Sicily, neither divorce nor separation was customary. Girls were brainwashed to believe that marriage was for life. No matter the problem, they worked through it or continued living unhappily. The whole town would know if a couple split up, and no one wanted to associate with a divorcee.

Staying married was the only option.

* * *

Nina risked her life to deliver her third daughter.

Two years after her second child, Lilly, was born, Nina learned there was another on the way. It was a difficult pregnancy.

Nina was placed on bed rest. Though she had her mother to assist, it pained her not to be able to help her little girls when they needed. Nina adored her daughters, and nothing meant more to her than being a devoted wife and mother.

Around the eighth month of her third pregnancy, Nina started hemorrhaging. Although her midwife should have recognized the problem before it got so bad, the woman had said nothing.

They rushed her to the hospital late that night for an emergency C-section.

Nina's midwife should have recognized the problem beforehand, but she'd said nothing lest she become unnecessary. Midwives were preferred for normal, healthy deliveries as a cheaper home-birth option. Hospitals were a luxury for those who could afford them or necessity for those with dangerous pregnancies.

Days later, Nina recuperated and was sent home with her newborn.

* * *

Mere months after their third child, Nicola decided to move to America.

He convinced Nina that he could make good money working construction in the US. He promised her that he would send enough back so she and the three children could live comfortably. There would be enough left for his own rent, food and a return ticket to Palermo. He would be back within the year.

But one year turned into three and a half, and Nina grew increasingly lonely.

It was like her husband had disappeared from the face of the earth with no way to reach him.

Chapter Three

There were no phone calls. There wasn't even a return address on the money Nicola sent.

Nina was scared, embarrassed, and finally humiliated that her husband had abandoned her and their children. The only person she confided in was the church pastor, who too suspected adultery. No man can stay away from his wife for so long without looking or engaging in other activities.

In a small town like this, few people minded their own business. The wise ones gossiped behind closed doors. The ignorant offered worthless advice.

Nina listened to one of the ridiculous suggestions and started preparing papers to acquire a visa from the U.S. Immigration Department in Palermo. Once she presented all the paperwork, however, she was denied.

The reason: Her husband had abused the system and stayed illegally in the U.S. after his 60-day visa expired.

The same ill-informed people then told her to try immigration in Naples, claiming they were more lenient and compassionate. Little did Nina know that once her husband's name was processed, the word *denied* would appear in red on their computer systems. All immigration officers throughout the embassies had the same information blocked.

Nina pleaded with them, saying they were separated and getting divorced. The agent informed her that when she returned with finalized divorce papers, only then would they process her application.

She was devastated. What was she going to do now?

Nina thought of her children. What would happen if Nicola stopped sending money?

One day, as she was hanging out clean laundry, one of the last people she wished to see appeared at her door.

It was the town's worst gossip. The woman was a wealth of misinformation.

She told Nina that she knew of her situation and that plenty of other women in town had the same abandonment story. The men left and never came back.

This was not what Nina wanted to hear. She politely listened before making an excuse, trying to get the woman to leave.

The gossiper got the message. However, before departing from Nina, the woman offered one final suggestion.

"There's a cruise starting from Naples to South America, stopping in Rio De Janeiro then Caracas, Venezuela, then onto Puerto Rico and ending in Miami. Why don't you go on that cruise, and see if in Miami they'll give you a 3-day visa to tour the city?"

Poor Nina listened with wide eyes, as if she could hear better that way.

"I'll think about it," she said, and thanked the woman.

Truthfully, Nina's mind had been made before the gossiper finished. She was getting on that cruise.

Nina went to bed excited, starting to believe that things could work out after all.

The following morning, she shared this excitement with her parents and sister. No one else needed to know.

Nina's mother didn't share her enthusiasm. She worried about the dangers.

What would her daughter and grandkids have to endure on this risky voyage? What would happen when Nina arrived at immigration in Miami? And lastly, what would her son-in-law's reaction be when he saw them? Would he welcome his wife and kids, support them, and have a place for them to stay?

Nina's mother wanted nothing but happiness for her daughter and grandchildren, but these unanswered questions tormented her. Many times, the elderly woman retired to bed only to endure a sleepless night, tears keeping her awake as she agonized over an uncertain future.

* * *

Meanwhile, Nicola Niceli had been reborn under a new American name—Nick.

Nick was making excellent money in construction.

He shared an apartment with two other Sicilian immigrants. They split the rent and utilities, except for food. He was earning four times what he'd made in Italy, more than enough to forgo returning home.

He thought about his kids more than his wife.

Nick had convinced himself that he was too young when he'd married Nina. He doubted he'd ever really loved her. It had only been the fleeting lust of a seventeen-year-old.

Chapter Four

One night Nick sat alone in his shared apartment. Thoughts of an encounter earlier in the day ran through his mind. He was now more convinced than ever that he had never loved his wife nor had he any desire for her.

So much had happened since he arrived in New York. True, the first six months were hard for him. The language barrier proved difficult. Nick missed the familiar faces from home. He kept getting lost in this big city. He worked six days a week, with only Sundays off. With little else to do, he spent his down time at home, relaxing and watching television shows he didn't understand.

But then things started getting better.

Nick learned how to stay afloat in New York City. He learned the streets and the subway system. He made friends through his job and by socializing at a nearby Italian café bar. In addition to Sunday, he got an additional day off during the week. He even purchased a used car. Obtaining the driver's license came easy for him. The written test for his permit was in Italian, and he passed the road test with flying colors.

Now up and around the city, Nick had decided to elevate his style. His type of work didn't require the best clothes—ripped jeans, T-shirts, and work boots were more appropriate for mixing wet cement and carrying heavy materials. He purchased more stylish clothing to wear on his days off, more confident about his location and finances. Next, he inquired about a good hairstylist in Brooklyn. He was fussy about his thick, curly hair, which he loved.

That was where he'd been earlier, getting a hair cut on his day off.

* * *

His friend had recommended a salon in Park Slope. It employed some of the top hair stylists for men, so Nick ventured out.

The minute he walked in, his eyes landed on one of the stylists.

Lightning struck.

"Have a seat," the owner of the salon said. He pointed to the very woman Nick had struggled to take his eyes from. "Carmen will take care of you in a minute."

Nick thought he'd hit the jackpot.

Carmen—wow, that's her name.

He waited for her to finish with her current customer. A feeling so powerful and intense that it couldn't be denied thundered within him. It cracked his chest open and spilled his soul out. It was turning him inside out, and there was no going back.

She called his name and gestured for him to sit in her chair.

Suddenly, the noise fled from the room.

All Nick heard as he walked over was the loud thump of his beating heart.

He sat down, forgetting why he was there. Was this a dentist appointment, or an eye doctor? He felt his body pressed against the chair, but the lightning had knocked away his awareness of anything more.

"How short do you want me to cut your hair?" Carmen asked. She had a slight accent, which made her even sexier.

Nick fixed his eyes to the large mirror in front of him. It was the only way to hide that he was staring at her. This way, he could look at every inch of her body without getting caught.

Carmen was a pretty little thing, with tight jeans, high heels, and long wavy black hair. She wasn't the typical girl you bring home to meet mamma. But she was the type every guy wants to bring home for himself.

Nick was smitten with the way she walked, the way she talked, even her cute accent. Everything about her, he loved. Her body, the clothes she wore, everything about her screamed sexy. Thoughts of her imprisoned his mind.

Carmen must have felt the same way about him, since she agreed to exchange phone numbers. Nick told her he'd call her on Saturday before saying goodbye.

* * *

Now, back in his apartment, Nick stared at the phone.

Why should I wait another four days before I call her?

He picked up the phone and dialed her number.

The ringing stopped as Carmen answered. Before she could speak, Nick said, "I know I told you I would call Saturday, but I just needed to talk to you. Am I calling you at a bad time?"

He worried she'd upset he'd called so soon.

Instead, Carmen said, "What took you so long?"

Relief washed over Nick, and a burst of loud laughter came out of his heart.

* * *

Nick and Carmen fell quickly for one another, and soon they'd become inseparable.

He would go to her apartment every day after work. The more he got to know her, the more he loved her. Carmen was very attentive to him; she made certain to give him all he needed. Nick returned home to a warm dinner, clean clothes, and the best in the bedroom. It wasn't long before he officially moved in.

Nick and Carmen acted like husband and wife. They went everywhere together and didn't care who might see them. She helped him get more work in the neighborhood and often would go with him to people's homes to look at a job and give appraisals. Whoever didn't know better assumed they were married. No one knew Nick had a wife and three children in Italy.

One day, Carmen's boss from the salon approached her. His sister and her husband, Tony, wanted to either remodel or put or in a new bathroom. The owner had recommended Nick. Carmen agreed.

Early Saturday evening, right after Carmen finished with her last customer, she and Nick drove to Tony's house. The first step was for Nick to look at the house and offer an estimate for either remodeling or building a new bathroom.

Upon arriving, the two were greeted with warm hospitality. Tony was an older man, also from Sicily. He was delighted to meet Nick and showered him admiration, especially when he saw Carmen.

"Your wife?" Tony inquired softly when Carmen wasn't listening.

"No, she's my girlfriend."

Tony, still warm and cheerful, joked, "So when will we eat these confettis?"

In Italy, white confetti almonds are typically given out at wedding celebrations. Tony didn't really care whether the two were engaged. He was only making conversation.

Nick just smiled.

Tony took the response to mean *one day*, and the topic was quickly dropped.

* * *

Carmen's birthday approached. Nick struggled to find the perfect gift. Their love had grown even stronger, and he wanted to make her happy.

She already had an abundance of jewelry. A new car would have been idea, but the sixty-thousand-dollar Mercedes she liked was out of the question.

What about a trip? It seemed the perfect answer, but Nick was worried. He'd started his own company. Though his employees were efficient, and generously paid, Nick had never left them to manage things without him. However, they reassured him things would go smoothly.

The next matter to determine was where to go. They'd always talked about Aruba, with its white sandy beaches, but that was out of the question. Nick needed to stay somewhere in the United States to avoid needing a passport or visa.

He racked his brain, and then he figured it out.

Puerto Rico.

Carmen had been born there and come to the U.S. as a teenager. The Caribbean island was her homeland, her heritage.

She's going to love it! But when and how should he surprise her?

* * *

While trying to figure out those details, Nick remembered that he knew someone living in Puerto Rico—his godfather.

In the Catholic tradition, godparents are chosen by the parents when a newborn is baptized. Nick's parents, Angelo and Maria Niceli, had chosen Carlo Stefano. At the time, he'd been married to Maria's cousin, and the families had been close. As a child, Nick had been very fond of his godfather.

Nick inquired after Carlo. The father of one of his employees turned out to have known him. From him, Nick learned more.

Carlo had moved to Puerto Rico after his wife, Giovanna, got sick and had changed his name.

"In Sicily, we knew him as Carlo Stefano, but now his name is Carlos Esteban."

The older man also remembered the names of Carlo's children, who had all moved to California. With this new information, Nick managed to get the number for Carlo's younger son, Charles. Prior to making travel arrangements, Nick gave him a call.

Charles didn't know Nick personally but remembered the stories his father would tell them about his favorite godchild.

"My father always spoke about you," Charles told Nick. He'd been delighted to hear that Nick wanted to get in contact with his father. "He will go nuts when he hears that you're in Puerto Rico. I'm sure he'd love to see you."

Despite the assurance, Charles was hesitant to give his father's address. Instead, he gave Nick his dad's phone number and a hint as to the location of his home.

"It's on a hilltop overlooking the Caribbean Sea in Cabo Rojo."

After Nick got all the information, he went to the travel agency and booked two airline tickets to San Juan. They were set to depart JFK on the morning of March 20, and they'd spend seven nights and seven days at La Paloma Beach Resort.

Carmen's birthday was two days earlier. Nick surprised her by taking her to her favorite restaurant, La Mexicana, near Lincoln Center. They had a delicious dinner along with sangria and margaritas. At the end of the meal, Carmen excused herself to go to the ladies' room. On her return to the table, she found a fresh glass of margarita and flan de coco displayed beautifully.

She also noticed an envelope underneath her dessert dish.

Carmen pulled it out and saw a typed itinerary, displaying the date of departure and return with no destination. Two tickets on a plane flying out of JFK in two days. Where to? It didn't say. Staying at? It didn't say that either.

"You'll find out once you get there," Nick told her.

There was also a card that read: *Pack island clothes and don't forget your bikini.*

Carmen was nearly exploding with joy.

* * *

The day before the trip, she was busy shopping for sundresses, bathing suits, and suntan lotion, but still had no idea of the destination. She begged over and over, asking Nick for a clue, but he wouldn't budge. His lips were locked and sealed.

"Fine, I don't want to know. I'll figure it out," she said, pouting as she left the room.

Curiosity was killing Carmen. She even went through his closet hoping to find a hint. Nick had planned everything so perfectly that she found nothing.

The following morning, the alarm clock rang at 5:00 a.m. She took a shower, dressed, and packed her toiletries. A half hour later they were out the door; an hour after that, they were pulling up to the curb at JFK.

The luggage was checked curbside. Nick held the boarding passes in his front shirt. The sign by the gate displayed only the flight numbers and departure times.

Carmen still had no idea which island in the Caribbean they were heading to. An announcement told them that it was time to board.

Nick and Carmen walked through the tunnel, ready to get on the plane. He was about two feet ahead, strolling like a cool cat. He turned to look at her with his devilish smile and said not a word.

Carmen fired back with squinted eyes. It was an expression that said *if looks could kill, you'd be dead right now*. Though it was all a playful game between the two of them, Nick was winning, and she was losing. Carmen hated to lose.

Nick's only goal was to surprise her.

Carmen sat by the window seat, looked around, and still couldn't find a clue.

When everyone was seated, the cabin doors closed. She buckled her seatbelt and complained that Nick's broad shoulders were invading her seat space. But she was only frustrated that she couldn't figure out where they were going. Secretly, she loved the feel of his tight upper arms against her, the scent of his cologne, even that he was trying to surprise her.

Nick knew that he'd succeeded in hiding the destination from Carmen. He gloated in the seat beside her until a voice over the loudspeaker revealed the truth.

"Good morning, this is Captain Donovan. Welcome aboard flight two eighty-nine. We have clearance for takeoff on runway six. Today's temperature is forty-eight degrees with clear skies. We're scheduled to depart on time at eight-thirty and arrive at San Juan Airport—"

Carmen's reaction was loud and involuntary. She screamed and clawed Nick's knee.

It hurt. Nick winced and gave her an embarrassed look.

As soon as Carmen composed herself, a big smile spread from ear-to-ear. She looked at Nick and softly whispered, "I love you."

"I'll love you too when you let go of my knee."

They shared a laugh as their plane took off, carrying the couple to their getaway.

Meanwhile, an ocean away, Nick's wife was planning a trip of her own.

Chapter Five

Nina was on her way to America.

It was early March of 1981, and she caught an early flight from Palermo to Naples with her daughters, Lilly and Gina. Her oldest daughter, Diana, remained in Sicily with her grandmother. It was best this way, for a few reasons—one, it was more economical; two, Nina's mother needed a grandchild around; and three, it meant one less extra mouth for Nicola to feed if they reached him.

Nina and her daughters traveled by boat. The twelve-day journey aboard a transatlantic cruise ship was fun and exciting for a young couple, a single person, or a family on vacation. But this was no typical cruise for Nina. She was traveling alone with two children aged six and four.

Their first days traveling across the Atlantic were torture. The sea was choppy and rough. At times, only blue water and sky were visible. Empty lounge chairs lined the outdoor deck.

Lilly and Gina were constantly seasick. Nina didn't feel much better, though she tried to stay strong for their sake. The smell of food from the main dining room didn't help their motion sickness. Nina tried to stay in the cabin, but she still had to venture out for food and water.

The experience was far from an ideal vacation.

*　*　*

When they docked in Rio de Janeiro, Nina was eager to step out on the main deck for fresh air but couldn't leave the kids alone. Little Gina had a fever, diarrhea, and was constantly vomiting—likely food poisoning or a viral infection, as if seasickness wasn't enough.

Luckily, during the ship's crossing, Nina had befriended an elderly Italian woman, Signora Anna, who came from a town near her own. The kind woman offered to stay with the sick girl so the others could briefly step out.

Grateful, Nina took Lilly, threw a sweater over her, and hurried down the long corridor to the stairs. She was afraid to take the elevator, but it hadn't occurred to her that she'd have to climb five flights to reach the deck.

By the time she arrived, Nina was exhausted and out of breath.

Looking over the railing into the crowded port proved less pleasurable than she'd imagined. Food carts billowed smoke. Crowds rushed in all directions. It was total chaos with no way to discern incoming from outgoing passengers.

Nina swiftly made her way back down, gripping Lilly's hand tightly.

Thank God, Gina was feeling better upon their return.

*　*　*

The next morning, the dining room smells were more tolerable. Nina decided to take the children there. It wasn't as bad as that first time, though they ate little and left quickly.

With the ship still moored in Rio de Janeiro, Nina and her daughters enjoyed a temporary respite from seasickness.

After breakfast, they visited the top deck. The girls passed the day playing happily.

"You count next, *Aurora*," Lilly said with a smile.

"Okay, *Bianca*," Gina agreed, covering her eyes.

Nina hid a smile as she heard them using the pretend names. Prior to leaving Italy, she'd instructed the girls to keep their real names secret. In reality, she thought it would be safer if no one knew their identities or their whereabouts. But she'd told her daughters it was a game. They had to obey if they wanted to win the biggest prize ever.

Luckily, Lilly and Gina loved it.

Their pretend names had been borrowed from Disney princesses. Nina had selected them herself: Bianca for the older girl, Aurora for the younger.

No one suspected they were fake—not even Nina's new friend, Signora Anna.

* * *

After departing Rio, their next stop was Caracas, Venezuela. The voyage took ten hours.

During the cruise, Nina had started trying to learn the meaning of the ship's long horn blasts, which it used to communicate with nearby vessels. A prolonged blast signaled their presence to other ships while repeat blasts meant a man overboard. There were many more signals to decipher.

The cruise arrived on schedule at the Caracas port early the next morning. Nina continued trying to make the best of their journey while managing the children's recurring illnesses.

Always in the back of her mind were fears centered on her husband.

Could Nina return home without him? She didn't have the option of taking her own life with two children to consider.

Perhaps, he still cares. Maybe we can work things out and start a new life in America together.

Nina clung to that slim possibility though she didn't believe it.

There were other things to consider. If denied a visa upon arriving in the U.S., could she escape customs? What if they shot at her or threw her in jail? What would happen to the children then?

Nina had to think with a clear mind.

The girls slept soundly in the cabin's one big bed. She shifted one, hoping to make space for herself and grab a couple hours rest before Caracas.

It was only after turning out the nightstand light that Nina realized they'd already arrived.

Sounds of commotion rose from the hallway. Cabin attendants searched for vacant rooms to clean. Most other passengers were up and about. A bus waited dockside to shuttle them to a beautiful beach barbeque provided by the crew.

A migraine throbbed behind Nina's eyes. How could she start this new day feeling so broken and shattered? She sat on the bedside, contemplating when a light knock came at the door.

A voice called to her. It was her new friend, the older Italian woman, Signora Anna.

Nina opened the door. Signora Anna was alert and dressed. She asked if Nina was ready yet.

Nina wanted to say no but thought of her children and how much fun the beach would be for them after being cooped up in the cabin.

"I'll be ready in fifteen minutes," she said.

Anna said it was a perfect sunny beach day.

"Great!" Nina forced a smile. "I'll just put their swimsuits on with shorts. I'll leave the shirts in my bag. What about breakfast for the kids?"

"There's plenty once we get to the bus," Anna responded reassuringly.

* * *

At the crowded Port of Caracas, Nina clung to Lilly's hand. She scanned the area and found the designated yellow bus with one orange stripe. Thrilled, the group of four hurried to it.

The woman in charge confirmed they were on the right bus and invited them to take food from a long table along the side. Baskets overflowed with freshly baked bread, rolls, croissants, and donuts. Plates displayed rows of ham and egg sandwiches. There were lines of boxed juices, platters of fresh fruit, and a full coffee service.

Grateful for the provisions, Nina packed extra in her bag for later.

The bus carried them to their designated beach area. Upon exiting, the children were given toys—a big red plastic pail, a shovel, jump rope, and large inflatable beach ball.

Lilly and Gina were delighted. But Nina was ecstatic. What mother wouldn't have been at the sight of her children's beaming smiles?

ABBANDONATA

The girls ran into the water the minute Nina removed their shorts, leaving just swimsuits. She shouted at them not to go in too deep. Then, to ease her mind, set a large towel a few feet from the water's edge.

Signora Anna joined her. The old woman had been a godsend to Nina. She'd helped with the children throughout this arduous trip, providing the warmth and support they'd previously gotten from their grandmother. Nina couldn't thank her new friend enough.

The sounds of her daughters splashing and laughing lightened Nina's mood. She enjoyed the warm sun, lying beside Signora Anna.

Preparations began for the barbeque feast. Latin music blasted from large speakers. The aroma of grilled meat spread across the beach. It brought Nina back to her childhood, when her world had been perfect. She had vivid memories of her family's country farmhouse, located on her father's property in the Bagheria countryside. It was a beloved summer retreat.

Each year, Nina had enjoyed fun-filled days and picnics by the lake. Her father took charge of the barbeque, while her mother prepared trays of food. The highlight was always the *pasta al forno*, which everyone eagerly anticipated. Another favorite was the large bowl of salad made from boiled string beans and potatoes, mixed with red onions, cucumbers, and tomatoes—an authentic Palermitano salad. Despite the inexpensive ingredients, Nina thought it was the best salad ever.

Nina stared into the distance, smiling as she lost herself in memories of the farmhouse.

"Daydreaming about something good?" Signora Anna asked.

Nina sighed. "The best memories ever."

She recalled when, as newlyweds, Nicola had joined her at these picnics. Though he'd vanished, her love for him remained, a deep flame burning in her heart.

Signora Anna rose and returned with two espressos. The two drank and shared stories about their hometowns.

"I have a brother who moved to America," Signora Anna shared. "His name is Carlo. He's retired now and living in Puerto Rico."

Nina was intrigued. She inquired more about Carlo's move to the U.S.

"His wife always dreamed of living in America," Anna explained. "My family cried for months after he left."

She hadn't seen her brother since his wife had passed away in 1970. For the rest of the family, it had been even longer. They hadn't seen Carlo since he'd left Sicily in 1959.

The bus arrived to return them to the cruise ship, and their day at the beach came to an end.

"Bianca! Aurora!" Nina called. The girls were still having a blast in the water. "It's time to clean up. We must leave the beach soon."

As Nina got the girls ready, Signora Anna continued sharing about her brother.

"He had over six godchildren," she recalled, though she didn't know their names.

Nina listened, interested but unaware of the connection. She'd never asked her husband who his godparents were.

Otherwise, she might have realized that Anna's brother, Carlo, was Nicola's godfather.

What a small world, indeed.

They boarded the bus and returned to the cruise ship in time to shower and change clothes for dinner.

As they entered the dining room, they noticed festive decorations.

"What do those mean?" Nina asked a waiter, pointing at the new décor.

"They're to celebrate our next stop," he explained. "We've set up a three-day excursion on the island of Puerto Rico."

Chapter Six

Nick and Carmen arrived at La Paloma Blanca Beach Resort. It was an enchanted vision of glistening white sand, like fresh snow on a meadow. The individual hacienda-type villas sat only a few feet from the azure water of the Caribbean. Around each villa was a wrap-around veranda of polished white wood with three steps leading to the sand.

Inside had two sections. One was an oversized living and dining room. A sheer white curtain separated the two halves. The living area featured a bar, flat-screen TV, and white leather sectional couch. The dining area was open, with only one wall at the far end and a table large enough to accommodate a party of twenty.

An arched door led to the bedroom. It looked like where a fairytale princess would sleep. Soft lace draped over the top of a four-poster canopy bed. Clusters of fuchsia hibiscuses cascaded down the posts. The organza fabric flowing down the posters was tied in the middle with a ribbon, creating a bubbly figure-eight. At night, the tie was released so guests could sleep in a chamber of heaven.

A platter of fresh tropical fruit waited for Nick and Carmen on the large table in the dining room.

They began settling in, admiring every detail of the resort. Carmen made two drinks before sitting on the couch. The material of her silk resort dress flowed across the cushions.

Nick joined her, taking one of the drinks. "So, do you like the place?"

"Gee, I don't know," Carmen responded, smiling. "I've got to think about it."

He jumped on her like a wildcat and pinned her down. "What do you mean *you've got to think about it*? This place is costing me an arm and a leg. You better modify your answer, bitch."

Carmen burst into laughter. She'd been teasing him, and he knew it all along.

Nick climbed off her and returned to his drink, enjoying the view. "Remind me to call my godfather tomorrow. He lives nearby, and I'm dying to see him. But today it's all about celebrating you, my delicious Puerto Rican *flan de coco*."

Nick and Carmen grabbed a bottle of champagne and two glasses, before moving to the prepared lounge chairs on the beach

The water lapped their feet. They absorbed the hot sun, played, and swam for most of the afternoon.

"We better get inside," Carmen said eventually. "I'm burning like a piece of meat."

Nick looked her up and down. "Yeah, babe, you're getting darker than me."

"That's impossible. When you were born you were already three shades darker than me."

Nick laughed. Her sarcastic remarks were part of what drove him crazy about her.

Barefoot, they walked back into their private heaven. They had a dinner reservation on the beach at six o'clock. Both settled in the bed for a quick nap first.

Carmen rose before Nick. She showered and started with her makeup and hair. Dressing properly for this dinner was her priority. His ten-minute preparation was a quick wash, putting on a pair of linen slacks with a matching shirt, and spraying a bit of cologne.

"Are you ready yet?" he asked, sitting in the living area.

"When I am ready, you'll figure that out by yourself. Stop rushing me! I'll be out as soon as I'm done."

"Did you major in sarcasm in college? Because you're awfully good at it. Oops, I forgot you didn't go to college." Nick laughed at his joke.

Although she was in the bedroom, Carmen heard every word he said. She smiled and continued to fix her hair. Moments later, she walked out into the living room where he was patiently waiting.

Nick got up from the couch and looked her up and down. He didn't say anything though. He wanted her craving his compliments.

Carmen placed her hands on her hips. "Well?"

"Well, what?"

"Well, what do you think?"

"Oh, you're ready? Yeah, you look okay."

Carmen's eyes narrowed, but there was a hint of concern in her glare.

"I'm teasing you babe," Nick said, bursting into laughter. He knew he'd conquered her and scored.

"You're such a prick."

Still laughing at his own victory, Nick finally offered her the words she'd wanted. "Okay, okay. You look and are so beautiful, my love."

"Please, tell me something I don't know," Carmen said, snubbing him by turning away with her nose in the air.

There went Nick's victory. *Bitch got me again.*

He took Carmen's hand.

Together, they walked barefoot on the pristine white sand. Not even a famous artist could have depicted such a beautiful night. The orange glow of the sun was about to set beyond the sea, while the white sand sparkled with the reflection of the candles on the beach. There was no breeze, just a comfortable stillness accompanied by the stars in the sky.

Nina would have given her whole life for a night like this with the man she loved so much. But Nick's heart had been stolen and imprisoned by Carmen, his Puerto Rican *flan de coco*.

Chapter Seven

The hem of Carmen's white transparent pants trailed across the sand. A hand-painted orange hibiscus blossomed on one leg.

Nick couldn't take his eyes off of her. The pants sat on her hips, paired with a crop top that left her stomach bare. Bell-shaped organza sleeves flowed over her wrists. His *coco de flan* was perfectly dressed for the Puerto Rican night.

Waiting for them on the beach was a table, set with fine China and three different sizes of stemware: a long, sexy flute for champagne, a wine glass, and a water glass. A linen napkin placed inside a woven basket kept the bread warm. Alongside the table, a shiny, stainless steel champagne bucket stood tall in the sand.

Nick and Carmen sat.

He poured and served her a tall flute of ice-chilled champagne.

A smile lit her face. "Oh Nick, you never cease to amaze me. You always outdo yourself and spoil me in so many ways."

Besides their conversation, the only sound was the soft waves, rolling back and forth from the ocean to the sand and then back again.

It was a magical evening, with delightful and delicious meals served to perfection. They both chose the famous *adobo mojado*, a succulent roasted pork that was seasoned and marinated. The tender meat fell off the bone.

Nick couldn't have been more satisfied with his dish.

They consumed three bottles of champagne before dessert: *flan de coco*, obviously. It was the best they'd ever had.

After dinner, they walked on the beach. Carmen noticed hammocks tied between two palm trees.

Holding his hand, like they were children, she asked, "Why are the palm trees swaying? Is there a light breeze, or is it the champagne making my head sway?" Either way, she felt intoxicated by it all.

Nick laughed. He held her as they walked on the sand. She barely made it to the first wooden step of their villa before feeling weak. He scooped her into his arms and carried her to their bed. He lay down next to her, stroking her hair until he too surrendered to a deep sleep.

* * *

The following morning, the sun peeked through the white shutters of the bedroom.

The light danced across the back of Nick's eyelids. He wasn't ready to see the sun yet. He squeezed his eyes tight and stretched his arm. His fingers brushed Carmen's soft, bare back. She must've gotten up in the middle of the night and undressed.

Nick snuggled closer to her. He stroked her soft face, lips, and shoulders with his index finger.

Like a kitten, she purred with delight. But Carmen didn't want to wake up yet.

It was now Friday morning. Nick knew that a waitress and a waiter would appear soon with trays of breakfast. He got up, allowing Carmen to sleep some more, and quickly showered, dressing in a pair of coral-colored shorts.

Not long after he finished, Carmen appeared by the bedroom door.

Nick's heart pounded as he took her in. She was the image of a Roman goddess.

"Good morning, my love. Why didn't my love wake me so we could've showered together?" Carmen teased.

Nick smiled. "Aww, don't tease me like that. Go back to bed and pretend you're still sleeping. I'll wake you up with kisses all over your body. Let me leave a note by the table on the veranda asking room service to leave breakfast for us there."

They both giggled at the idea.

"No," Carmen said. "It's okay, Nick, I don't like cold eggs for breakfast. I'll take a raincheck and won't forget to use it."

She retreated to the bathroom, appearing ten minutes later wrapped in a pair of towels. The larger one held her hair, but her body was covered by a much smaller piece of fabric.

Nick didn't pretend not to stare. Heat flowed through him. He was so turned on by the sight of her that he considered locking the door and pouncing on her after all.

A loud knock ruined his plan.

Nick tried to clear his mind, but he couldn't shake his disappointment in the interruption.

A waiter and waitress stepped into the villa. He rolled a cart with a tray of the best tropical fruit, all cleaned and sliced; a silver-plated pot of fresh-brewed Colombian coffee; a decanter filled with fresh passion fruit juice; and two small stainless-steel domes holding warm scrambled eggs with bacon. She carried a basket of hot croissants and fresh waffles, covered with a linen napkin to keep them warm.

Nick and Carmen enjoyed their breakfast then moved to lounge on their couch. They discussed their trip and made plans for their next five days in Cabo Rojo. Carmen wanted to visit a jewelry maker to look at the coral. There, they could choose coral extracted from the sea and decide what kind of jewelry to have it set in.

"Okay, yeah," Nick said. "Why not? I'll go to the main office of the resort and make arrangements. But first, my sweet Carmen, I have to call my godfather."

Despite his insistence, Nick remained slow to act, making excuses. *Maybe Carlo gets up late. I don't want to wake him up.* An hour had passed before Nick finally lifted the phone.

The paper with the number trembled in his hand.

"Jesus Christ almighty!" Nick set the paper down and looked at Carmen, watching him from the couch. "Why am I so nervous to make this call? I haven't seen or talked to him in twenty-five years, but I was a kid then. He left Sicily when I was ten years old."

He continued to procrastinate, sharing details about his godfather: how he'd changed his name from Carlo Stefano to Carlos Esteban, how he'd moved to Puerto Rico after his wife's death, how he'd baptized Nick when he was an infant.

Eventually, there was nothing more to tell.

Nick picked up the phone again and began to dial. He leaned against the couch, trying to be cool and relaxed. In reality, he was more nervous than a father in the maternity ward. His foot tapped against the floor. He took deep, heavy breaths like he'd been blowing up balloons.

The phone rang twice. Nick hoped no one was home. But, before the third ring, a male voice answered, "*Hola, esta es la casa de Señor Esteban. ¿Puedo preguntar quién llama?*"

Nick didn't speak Spanish, but he recognized the name. He'd reached the right home.

Perhaps if he spoke slowly, the person on the other end would understand him.

"*Mi chiamo Nick Niceli,*" he said, introducing himself in Italian before asking to speak with his godfather. "*Desidero parlare con Carlo Esteban.*"

No response came.

Nick had learned only a couple words of Spanish before making this trip. This was a chance to use them. He tried to explain his relationship to Carlo.

"*Soy su ahijado.*" Nick sounded out each syllable for the Spanish word for *godson*. Then, he attempted to provide more context. "*Soy de Bagheria, Sicilia.*"

Silence again.

Nick worried he'd messed up somehow. But the man on the other end understood. He shouted to *Señor Esteban* to come and speak. A more mature voice responded. This one was soft-spoken and deliberate, the better to avoid mistakes.

There was a shuffling sound, like a phone being handed over. Then, deep, expectant breaths.

To make his godfather more comfortable, Nick spoke first, switching to his familiar Sicilian dialect.

"Hello, *parrinu*. It's me, your *figghiocciu*."

Upon hearing those words—godfather and godson—spoken in his own dialect, Carlo became emotional, sobbing and struggling to respond.

Nick was touched. *Maybe I should have been there in person so I could have hugged and comforted him.*

The man who'd first answered the phone spoke in the background, comforting Carlo. From the overheard snippets of conversation Nick concluded that this man was Felipe, his godfather's loyal companion and butler.

Composure regained, Carlo managed to get out a question. "Where are you?"

"We're staying at La Paloma Blanca Beach Resort."

"Here in Cabo Rojo?"

"Yes," responded Nick, "here in Cabo Rojo."

A big hearty laugh came from the old man. "Nicola Niceli, you have chosen the resort I own."

"Wow." It was the only word Nick could manage.

"What brings you here, Nicola?" Carlo asked.

"I go by Nick now, *parrinu*," he explained, grinning from ear to ear. "I have a dear and beautiful girlfriend who I adore. It just so happens it was her birthday a couple of days ago. I surprised her with this trip since she is a native Puerto Rican. Where else to take her but here?"

Carlo laughed.

"I also heard that you'd retired here on the island, so I asked around and got your son's number. He told me how to contact you, but he wouldn't give me your address. He said, *If my father wants to see you, he'll give you the address.*" Nick chuckled.

"So, he's pretending to care about his old man," Carlo growled. "If they cared so much, they wouldn't be living so far away from me in California. That's a story I'll tell you one day."

Nick continued, "Your son mentioned you were somewhere in Cabo Rojo, so I made sure the travel agency got us into a resort in the area."

"So you booked a surprise trip for your girl but made sure it was in Cabo Rojo to see me?"

"What do you think, *parrinu*? Of course!"

The old man felt a glow in his heart, hearing his godson talk so affectionately after so many years. "We have so much to talk about, Nick. I am so honored and happy that you looked for me. I haven't felt this happiness in a long, long time. We have to catch up on twenty years of absence."

Nick's earlier anxiety proved unfounded. They spoke for a while, offering tidbits about their lives since leaving Italy.

Carlo extended the warmest invite. "I'll leave you free tonight, but tomorrow morning, my driver will come and pick you up. Make sure you bring your girl."

At no point in their exchange had Nick mentioned that he had a wife and kids in Sicily. Carlo had no idea.

Nick hung up the phone with a big smile.

He explained to Carmen, who hadn't understood a word of the conversation. "Do you know that this godfather of mine, Señor Carlos Esteban, is one of the wealthiest men in Puerto Rico? He owns a luxury resort here."

"Oh my God, Nick! We should've gone to the one he owns!"

Nick squinted, trying to get a better picture of her expression. "Baby, you're sitting right in it."

"What the hell are you saying? He owns La Paloma?"

"Yup, and God knows what else he owns."

Carmen was too stunned to speak.

"He also has eight of the best thoroughbreds in the world," Nick continued, eager to relay everything he'd just learned. "He imported them from England. They're trained for racing. Plus, he owns three beautiful white horses and two palominos with golden coats and blond manes, all for horseback riding on his estate. Just for pleasure."

With each piece of information, Carmen's eyes grew wider.

"And the best part, my dear Carmen, is that tomorrow morning, his chauffeur will pick us up and drive us to his estate. Be ready by nine-thirty. The driver will be here by ten sharp and will meet us in the reception area."

* * *

Over on his estate, Carlo summoned a meeting with his entire staff in the large formal dining room. All his servants lived on the property in a detached two-story building. Eight of them in total lived in on the property with him—his private chef, two housekeepers, two chauffeurs, the stableman, his groundskeeper, and, of course, Felipe, his long-time loyal friend and butler.

All eight of them gathered around Carlo as he informed them about the preparations to be made. He was expecting a visit from not one, but two, beloved family members from his past: his godson and his sister, Anna.

A message had come from Anna a few days prior. She was on a cruise that would be stopping in Puerto Rico and was overjoyed at the prospect of seeing him. Carlo shared his sister's excitement.

Now, with his godson on the island as well, Carlo had twice the reason to celebrate.

He would soon have the chance to host both his godson and his sister on his property.

Chapter Eight

The following morning, Nick and Carmen arrived at the main house early, hoping to have a quick breakfast. To their surprise, however, one of Carlo's drivers, Carmelo, was already there. He sat in the front of a Bentley, waiting for his employer's beloved godson.

"I was hoping you'd be late, so we could've eaten or at least had a cup of coffee," Nick admitted as they climbed in, and took off toward the estate.

Feeling guilty, Carmelo picked up the phone in the car and called the house.

Felipe answered with his usual greeting. "*Hola, esta es la casa de—*"

"*Soy yo.*" Carmelo interrupted. "*Puedo decirle a Dante para preparar un delicioso desayuno completo para dos?*"

At the estate, Felipe sent this message to Dante, who began preparing a full, delicious breakfast for two.

As the car approached, Nick and Carmen stared at the lush tropical flowers and 40-foot palm trees that lined the mile-long cobblestone driveway. An iron, oval plaque hung over a massive red gate at the end, naming the estate: *Castillo de Esteban*.

* * *

The Bentley approached a circular path made of small white cobblestones. In its center, an orchard of lemon trees perfumed the air. The citric scent greeted Nick and Carmen as they stepped out the car.

Carmelo had stopped in front of two arched, rustic wooden doors with massive iron handles.

The sight reminded Carmen of the novel *Scarface*. She leaned close to Nick and whispered, "This is a fortress. Are you sure Tony Montana doesn't live here?"

Nick grinned, trying not to laugh.

Inch-by-inch, the massive doors creaked open. Felipe, the butler, stood on the other side.

Behind Nick and Carmen, Carmelo yawned. "What took you so long to open the doors, Felipe?"

The butler glanced at him but ignored the question. Felipe lived by the rule *silence is golden*. He only spoke to welcome Nick and Carmen to *la Casa de Esteban* before guiding them to the foyer.

A grand circular staircase spiraled upward. Descending its steps was a tall, handsome man with slightly white hair—Carlo Stefano, turned Carlos Esteban.

Nick ran forward before catching himself. He wasn't a child anymore. Proceeding at a brisk walk, he approached his godfather and wrapped him in a tight embrace. "*Parrinu*, what a pleasure to see you."

Carlo, speechless, but with watery eyes, replied, "My God, how long have I desired to see you here."

"Well, you've got me here now," Nick said.

Both smiled broadly.

Nick took Carmen's hand and introduced her to his godfather, still speaking in Sicilian. "*Parrinu*, this is the woman who completes me."

"Bravo! What is this doll's name?"

"Her name is Carmen."

Struggling to keep up with the Italian, Carmen nudged her boyfriend. "Okay, I understood that last part, but what did you say before that?"

"Oh, that?" Nick replied.

"Yeah, that," she said sarcastically.

"I told him you're a professional hooker, and I picked you up on the streets of New York," Nick joked, laughing.

Carmen turned beet red. "Oh, wait till I get your balls tonight."

This could have gone on, but they were interrupted by Carlo.

"Let me show you the house," he said, speaking Sicilian. "No, wait! I heard you haven't had breakfast! Dante's prepared a meal for you. Go ahead to the dining room. Felipe will guide you. I need to go to the stables and talk to Juan, my stableman, but I'll meet you guys in the patio of the dining room in thirty minutes, okay?"

* * *

"That was the most delicious breakfast I've ever had," Carmen said. "The fresh fruit platter looked like would take forever to prepare. How did the chef have all this ready for us?"

Nick nodded, sharing her surprise. "Did you eat the chilled papaya?" he asked. "I think they grow them here on the property. I saw trees of yellow and orange papayas as we drove up. The fresh oranges are from here too."

"No wonder those mimosas were so good."

They laughed and rose from the large table. Hand-in-hand, they walked to the covered patio, which connected to the main dining room by a pair of arched doors that slid into the walls when open.

Nick and Carmen both stared in wonder. Before them was a gorgeous swimming pool. It had been constructed so that a natural freshwater waterfall, formed by rocks over a hundred years ago, cascaded into the pool. It created an infinity effect. They couldn't see where it ended and where the ocean began. It looked like a flatbed of blue water.

Carlo called to them and waved them over. He sat at a round mosaic-tiled table. The ring showed miniature lemons, while the middle shone a brilliant azure, matching the Caribbean water.

In the corner of the open patio, behind Carlo, was a large dome wood-burning pizza oven. It matched the mosaic tiles in the center of the table. The oven rotated as it baked and could handle up to ten pies at a time.

"So, *Caramella*," Esteban asked, as the pair joined him at the table. "How did you manage to capture the heart of my devilish godson?"

Carmen turned to Nick and whispered, "Did he just call me *Caramella*, like the candy?"

"I think so," Nick responded.

Carmen looked straight at Esteban and pointed her index finger up and down. "I knew I was going to like you. As far as the capturing goes, all it took was one look from me, and he was captured. He's the one who had to work on capturing my heart."

"Ouch, *molto caliente* and *confident*," Esteban teased.

Carmen giggled. She didn't speak Italian, but his response had been close enough to Spanish for her to understand.

The conversation moved on, and Carlo explained the layout of the rest of the house.

"Four of the primary bedrooms have their own balcony, a walk-in closet, a jacuzzi, and private baths and showers. They can fit eight adults, but in my house, only two at a time is sufficient." Carlo laughed. "The other four bedrooms have king-size beds and private bathrooms."

Soon, the conversation changed to stories from the time they'd spent apart. Nick still didn't mention his wife and children in Sicily.

They were served afternoon cocktails. Nick and Carmen had passion fruit mojitos. Carlo had his usual prosecco sorbet mimosa.

The old man took a sip and leaned back in his chair. "How long are you staying on the island?"

"We arrived on Thursday the twentieth and should return home on the twenty-seventh, next Thursday," Nick replied.

Carlo was saddened. "But today is the twenty-second. I only have you for another four days. We have to make some changes here."

Nick smiled, amused but respectful, and let the old man finish his thought.

"First and foremost, you guys won't have to stay at La Paloma Beach Resort anymore."

Carmen wanted to object. *No, I love that place!* But she sipped her mimosa and held her tongue, already fond of the old man.

"Your full amount will be refunded. And, for the rest of your visit, I would love for you to stay here. You can have the presidential suite, which used to be my private quarters before my Signora passed. If you liked La Paloma Blanca, you'll find it shabby compared to what I'm offering."

Then, perhaps remembering that he was speaking to a couple, Carlo gave an alternative.

"Or, if you desire more privacy, I have a small, enchanted villa, less than a quarter mile down the road on my property. It's near the water with a wrap-around porch. You'll have a cook, a chauffeur, and a cleaning lady daily. How can you refuse that?"

Nick couldn't. His godfather had always treated him like a son. Nick loved Carlo too much to turn down any of his requests. The fact that the old man now lived alone melted Nick's heart.

Still, he had to consider Carmen's opinion.

Nick turned to her and whispered. "What do you think? I feel so bad—"

Carmen cut him off. "If you don't accept, I'll beat you to a pulp. Your godfather is so adorable and affectionate. I can't believe how attached I've become to him in less than an hour."

"So does that mean it's a yes?"

"Of course, and if you want to go, I'll stay here by myself."

Nick couldn't contain his joy. He burst out laughing.

Carlo soon joined in when he learned they would stay. Though shorter than his godson, the old man wrapped his arm around Nick's broad shoulders. Then, without hesitation, he grabbed Carmen's shoulder, embracing her as well.

She squeezed his hand tightly in return.

The happy trio returned inside. Carlo intended to give them a tour of his house. However, Felipe waited for him in the dining room.

A phone call had come in from a ship near Puerto Rico.

"That's Anna!" Carlo shouted, excited. He excused himself and hurried to the library to take the call.

Carlo's heart soared with joy as he listened to his sister's voice.

"Of course, I'm planning to visit," she assured him. "But I have a friend aboard with me I'd like to bring. She's a mother with two young children. They'll have to come too."

"Of course, you can bring them!" Carlo was too thrilled at the thought of seeing his siter to deny her any request. "It's a pleasure for me to welcome them. It will be refreshing to see young ones running around the house."

"Thank you a million times, my dear brother."

"You don't need to thank me. You're my sister, my family, my blood. *Sangu mio*." It was a loving expression that their parents had often used. Both siblings grew emotional at hearing it again.

Wanting to avoid getting too worked up while on the phone, Anna changed the topic. "Carlo, don't mention that I have already called. I'll call you again tomorrow morning, and I'll bring the young mother with me. Her name is—"

Before Anna could say more, the phone line went dead.

* * *

On the ship, several hundred miles away, Anna visited Nina's cabin after her conversation with her brother. They each sat on at an end of the large bed.

"You just have to come with me to my brother's house," Anna said. "I know he'll be more than happy to have someone from Bagheria."

"I feel like I'd be intruding. I don't know him, and besides, showing up with two children doesn't sit well with me."

Anna understood but refused to accept Nina's objection. "No, no. You're coming with me, and that's final. It will be lovely, you'll see."

* * *

Carlo returned to Nick and Carmen, his face red with excitement and joy. He looked at his godson, took a deep breath, and said, "Nick, tomorrow I get to see my sister after so many years. Can you imagine how I feel right now? To have her and you here in my home at the same time?"

Nick smiled. "Is she coming by plane?"

"No," Carlo said. "She took a cruise from Naples, and one of the destinations is here in Puerto Rico for three days. I have invited her to stay here with me, and she's bringing a Sicilian woman with her kids to spend three days with us as well."

An excited Carlo resumed the tour of the house that had been interrupted. As he walked ahead, Nick leaned close and whispered to Carmen, "These ladies must have money like Carlo. Who takes a cruise from Italy all the way to the Caribbean?"

"Who cares how rich they are? We'll probably meet them if they're coming in tomorrow," Carmen said.

And, for the time being, the matter was dropped.

Chapter Nine

After completing the tour of the Castillo, Carlo had one of his drivers take Nick and Carmen to the beautiful villa by the beach.

When they reached their enchanted new vacation home, they felt welcomed by the breathtaking view of the luxurious property. The stunning architecture and intricate details left them speechless. It had all the amenities of a mansion but on a smaller scale.

Carlo had been right. An invitation to stay there was impossible to refuse.

"Let's not get too used to this," Nick said, staring at the luxury surrounding them. Their life in Brooklyn was nothing so glamorous.

But they couldn't resist the excitement of exploring the villa. Carmen opened what she thought was a bathroom door and instead discovered a jacuzzi surrounded by statues of goddesses. A dome-shaped clear glass ceiling allowed sunlight to shine through, creating an iridescent effect on the room's azure tiles.

The villa featured a curved kitchen with a half-round island equipped with six stools and a dining area with a rectangular table large enough for eighteen, and a family room with a blue-trimmed white sofa. This curved couch was accented by yellow and blue suede pillows and faced a flat-screen television that had been mounted to the wall. Below the screen was a built-in cabinet filled with Carlo's rare and expensive French cognacs and champagnes.

Nick opened a door that led to a spectacular primary bedroom, once occupied by Carlo and his wife, Giovanna. French glass doors led to a private balcony overlooking the water. There were four other bedrooms in the circular hallway and dome.

Nick and Carmen were in awe.

"I don't think I ever want to leave this place," she said, staring at the ocean from the patio. She leaned against Nick's chest. "Let's get our things at La Paloma so we can sleep here tonight."

"We can't leave without going back to the house and telling Carlo," Nick reminded her. "It wouldn't be the right thing to do."

* * *

Carmelo leaned on the Jeep, waiting for their return.

"I didn't know you were waiting for us," Nick apologized.

"I know what you meant to my *padrone*, Señor Nick." Carmelo said. "I would have waited much longer, even if I wasn't told."

"You're a good employee, Carmelo," Nick said. "But you don't have to call me *señor*."

"Thank you, señor."

* * *

It was close to seven o'clock when they returned, and the patio was set for dinner. Nick and Carmen sat at their places beside the old man.

"Tell me something, Carlo," Carmen said with her usual sweet demeanor. "Are you always this considerate and sweet?"

Carlo laughed, then looked straight at her.

For a second, Carmen wondered she'd said something wrong.

"My sweet *Caramella*, you told me it took one look from you to capture Nick's heart. That same look has captured mine, but in a fatherly way. Have I explained myself, young lady?"

"You have," she said. "And the same goes for me. You've captured my heart in that way too."

"Enough of this mushy stuff!" Nick said, waving his napkin at them before placing it over his knees. "What am I, chopped liver?"

"You know very well what you mean to me," his godfather assured him.

They enjoyed a delicious dinner. Dante had outdone himself with perfectly roasted, succulent pork accompanied by yuca and *escalivada*, a mix of roasted vegetables.

Their meal was accompanied by wine drawn from a barrel in the estate's *cantina*. Nick and Carmen had visited the below ground-level room on their tour. It stored all the wine barrels and salamis, keeping them cool.

After dinner and dessert were finished, they were served Carlo's special rum, *chichaito de coco*, in tall, sexy glasses.

Their conversation turned to Carlo's joy at seeing his sister tomorrow.

"So, who's this young mother she's bringing?" Nick asked.

"I don't know," Carlo said. "She was about to tell me her name when all of a sudden the phone died. They were on the cruise ship together, and my sister invited her and her kids to come along. That's all I know."

They must be rich friends who planned this expensive trip together, Nick thought. He had no idea how wrong his assumption would be.

As it got late, they said their goodnights. A new driver, Luca, waited to take them back to Paloma.

"I'll be expecting you guys to move into my beach house tomorrow?" Carlo confirmed.

"Yes, most definitely," Nick assured him.

Carmen inhaled the intoxicating scent of the flowers along the driveway, smiling the entire drive.

Chapter Ten

The cruise ship was scheduled to dock in Puerto Rico at mid-afternoon on Sunday, March 23rd.

That morning, before breakfast, Signora Anna invited Nina to accompany her to the captain's quarters. She said she needed to call her brother.

Nina assumed that her friend wished to remind him of their imminent arrival in Puerto Rico. However, Anna had other plans.

After telling her brother about the details about their scheduled arrival, she turned the conversation to Nina.

"Carlo, my dear brother, I would like to bring a sweet guest from Sicily with her two little girls. She feels nervous because she doesn't know you and is hesitant about accepting my invitation. Will you please talk to her and assure her she's welcome in your home?"

"Put this Sicilian girl on the phone," Carlo replied. "And tell her she won't refuse this Siciliano."

Nina was caught off guard. She hadn't expected to be mentioned and at once felt as though she'd been put on the spot. Refusing to talk to Anna's brother would make things even more awkward. Reluctantly, she took the phone.

"*Ciao, sugnu Nina,*" she said, introducing herself.

The minute the old man heard her speaking in Sicilian, he grew emotional, pouring his heart out to her. "It's more than an honor to welcome somebody from my hometown whose clothing still smells like my homeland. Please give me the honor of having you and your children in my home. I live alone with my housekeepers. My children are both married and live in California. I see them maybe once every two years. My wife has passed, so having your company and my sister will give me the greatest pleasure. I also have my godson here. He comes from our neck of the woods too. Having you all here is like Christmas morning for me. Your little girls will each have their room filled with toys and new clothes. We'll make this a Christmas morning for all."

How could Nina refuse such kindness?

"I will be more than happy to accept your invitation," she replied and handed the phone back to a beaming Signora Anna.

* * *

That same Sunday morning, Nick and Carmen left La Paloma Blanca Beach Resort for their new home on Carlo's property.

They settled in, feeling a bit exhausted. After their dinner the night before, the two had stayed up reminiscing on the couch, discussing Carlo and the new guests that would be joining them.

Carmen stretched out along the curved sofa. Voice tinged with anticipation, she asked, "What are we doing for lunch?"

As if on cue, Dante knocked on the door.

"Come in," Nick shouted.

The chef entered and informed them that he'd brought their lunch. He set two large trays with dome covers on the table. Then, with the help of a young girl he'd brought to assist, Dante lifted in a wooden box, filled with homemade wine, bottles of spumante, and snacks for them to enjoy throughout the day.

After setting the table and displaying all the food, Dante took his leave.

This time, the meal was Nick's favorite: grilled seafood marinated in garlic sauce, accompanied by a plain fennel salad with slices of oranges. It reminded him of dishes from Sicily. He suspected his godfather had selected the meal.

He's unbelievable. What a fine, quality man!

To Nick's delight, Dante had also prepared barbecued swordfish *spitini*, better known as swordfish *rollatini*, featuring slices of swordfish stuffed with seasoned breadcrumbs and rolled onto wooden skewers, and then barbecued. A basket of freshly baked bread completed the spread.

Both Nick and Carmen indulged in a full pitcher of white wine sangria, garnished with fresh wedges of peaches. Carmen was soon feeling the effects, and her words began to slur. Nick couldn't help but laugh at her charmingly tipsy state. Seeing her like this brought him nothing but pleasure.

Carmen tried to walk but fell on the couch like a slippery eel.

Nick scooped her up, got her seated upright, and covered her with a blanket.

She'll sleep it off. Just a couple of hours, that'll fix her.

* * *

It was approaching evening by the time Carmen woke. She yawned and stretched like a cat. Then, the dryness of her mouth hit her.

"I'm so thirsty! Oh Jesus, I'm dying of thirst!"

Carmen peeled herself off the couch, eyes mostly closed. She stumbled to the kitchen island where a second pitcher of sangria stood. Dante had prepared it for later in the evening.

Mistaking it for water, Carmen gulped down a tall glass. The cool drink quenched her thirst. Without realizing what she was doing, she downed another glass.

This time, the alcohol hit her hard.

* * *

Nick shoved Carmen, trying desperately to wake her. It was almost seven-thirty pm. She'd been out for hours.

"Babe, come on, we promised Carlo we'd be there for dinner. His sister and that young mother are probably there already. Please, get up!"

But his pleading had no effect. Seeing that it was useless, he slumped onto the couch and called his godfather.

"I'm afraid we can't make it tonight," Nick apologized. "Carmen is ill."

"Don't worry, Nick," the deep voice replied. "I understand. Just take care of *Caramella*."

His godfather's compassion made Nick feel even worse.

* * *

Meanwhile, at dinner on Carlo's estate, Nina couldn't stop praising the food. It was just like what she'd eaten in Bagheria.

"*El Padron Esteban* requested this special dinner," Dante confessed to her.

Nina should have suspected it had been the Sicilian old man's idea. It was as though she'd returned home.

Between the food, the conversation in Sicilian dialect, and the climate, Puerto Rico feels a lot like Bagheria, she thought.

Lilly and Gina were overjoyed as well. Carlo had welcomed them with gifts of toys, jewelry, and beautiful clothes handpicked by the best stylists. Among them had been two special boxes, beautifully wrapped in hot pink and Tiffany blue. Inside them had been the latest bathing suits for little girls, with matching sandals and sun hats.

Having finished his conversation with Nick, Carlo returned to the table. He watched the young mother and her daughters, intrigued. He inquired about her relatives in Bagheria.

Although Nina already felt a strong connection to the old man, she was afraid to tell him her full story.

What would he think of her crossing the Atlantic with two small children, not knowing if they'd even be allowed to enter the U.S, all to get back her husband?

Nina told him everything about *her* side of the family. She mentioned no husband, nor any of Nick's relatives.

For his part, Carlo knew that the children must have had a father. But since Nina didn't mention her husband, he decided not to pry lest it make her uncomfortable.

When she's ready, he thought, *she'll tell me.*

***

After dinner, Felipe and Signora Anna accompanied Nina and the children. The butler opened the doors to the bedroom where the girls were to stay.

Nina found herself lost for words.

Six porcelain dolls, each dressed in a beautiful outfit, sat around a princess-style bed. On either side, a small, pink and lavender wooden table with four matching chairs displayed a polka dot porcelain tea set.

One for each girl, Nina thought.

Lilly and Gina rushed toward the toys. Their happiness was surpassed only by their mother's own. Nina felt doubly joyful, experiencing the delight of each of her daughters.

Once the girls were washed and dressed in their new silk pajamas, Nina, Signora Anna, and Felipe left them through a pair of French double arch doors. These connected to Nina's own room.

Once she stepped through, Nina let out a delighted sigh. "Oh my goodness! Have I died and gone to heaven?"

The room was filled with top-quality furnishings. Nina had never owned nor witnessed such luxury before.

An antique curved dresser at the foot of the bed caught her eye. It was hand-painted with white baby's breath and ferns on the corners. The center depicted two angels with pink peonies clustered by their feet. It was unbelievably gorgeous.

Above Nina was a dome-shaped ceiling. Like the dresser, it had been hand-painted with angels, white clouds, and a spectacular fresco of Michelangelo's "Creation of Man."

Nina wondered if the Sistine Chapel could compare to this beauty.

Truly, Carlo was a Renaissance man, deeply religious and humble despite his wealth.

Nina opened an antique curved dresser to find a flat-screen television, positioned to be enjoyed while lying in the bed.

"How do they think to come up with such luxury?" Nina asked.

Signora Anna shrugged, equally puzzled. "Don't ask me, my dear girl. I come from the same neck of the woods as you."

Both ladies laughed.

The stone-faced Felipe excused himself with a curt goodnight and exited the room.

"I think I should retire too," Signora Anna said. "It's getting late. But first, I want to go back downstairs and see my brother again."

* * *

That night, Nina lay in bed, dressed in a long silky nightgown and admiring the ceiling. She wished her husband was there to enjoy this experience.

"What drove you away?" she whispered.

Suddenly, in the comfort and privacy of the room, tears rolled down Nina's cheeks.

She buried her face in the pillow to muffle her cries, but she was uncontrollable and couldn't stop.

Where are you, Nick? What did I do to you? Why do I still love you so much?

He'd abandoned her, yet she'd come all this way to search for him. Was she a glutton for punishment or too foolish to let him go? Did she have no pride? Or did she have too much, and it had blinded her and made it impossible for her to face the town alone?

All these worries ran through Nina's mind.

"He doesn't love me, nor does he desire me." The tears continued, faster and louder than before. Nina squeezed her eyes shut, trying to stop them. "Still, I have to face him and have him tell me."

With that final thought, Nina rolled onto her side. Quietly, her sobs turned to sleep.

* * *

In the main dining room below, Carlo and Anna shared some warm cognac.

"Is she married?" the old man asked his sister. "If she has a husband, where the hell is he?"

Anna could only provide her brother with the little information she knew.

"I don't understand why a young mother would go on a cruise all by herself with two children." Carlo rested his glass down.

Anna sipped her cognac. "Perhaps she'll feel more comfortable and share more of her story tomorrow."

"Listen, my dear sister, something is wrong. That poor child is carrying a heavy cross." Carlo sighed, staring up toward the ceiling and Nina's room above. "It's not that I want to know because I'm nosy. I'm not. But she tugs on my heart. I think, what if she were my daughter? What would I do?"

Feeling himself grow emotional again, the old man took a sip of his cognac. It did little to calm him. But there was more he needed to say, so he took a deep breath, met his sister's eyes, and continued.

"Then, I look at her daughters, and another question pops up."

"Their names?" Signora Anna guessed.

"Yes!" Carlo slapped his hand on the table. "Sometimes, they forget to answer to them. Don't you find?"

"*Biancaneve* and Aurora are princess names," Signora Anna said. "I suspect the girls have different ones and are only pretending, but I haven't said anything. I don't want to embarrass Nina if she isn't ready to share."

"No," Carlo agreed. "But it makes me worried. The poor girl must be terrified if she's hiding her children's names."

"Perhaps she thinks that news of their arrival will spread in New York and her husband might run away before she can find him if he hears all three of them are coming."

A dark expression twisted Carlo's face. The kind old man vanished, and his fist tightened around his glass. "Only the worst kind of pig would run from his children like that. He'd deserve the worst kind of punishment."

Suddenly nervous, Signora Anna rested her hand on her brother's own to calm him. She understood—better than any of the other guests on the estate—that these were not empty words.

From a man as powerful as Carlo, his statement was a threat.

Chapter Eleven

The Monday morning sun was perfect for a swim in the pool.
Nina walked through the arched doors into her daughters' room. Lilly and Gina were still in bed, playing happily with their new dolls.

"Who wants to go swimming in that big, beautiful pool?" Nina asked, jumping into the center of the bed with them.

The girls screamed with joy. "I do! I do!"

"Perfect. Put your new swimsuits on, and we'll go downstairs to meet Signora Anna and Señor Carlos for breakfast on the patio."

Nina helped them dress, then turned to fix the bed.

"Signora Nina, please," a woman's voice called to her suddenly from by the door. In Spanish, she continued, "You don't need to do the beds. We are here to do all the chores."

Nina, who spoke only Italian, didn't understand. However, she recognized her name and turned. Two women stood in the doorway. These were Lucia and Paloma, Carlo's housekeepers.

Despite the language barrier, the two made their intentions clear. At their insistence, Nina let go of the pillow she'd been fluffing and stepped away from the bed. She watched for a few moments, amazed as the two housekeepers hurried to fix everything.

Wow. Even in my wildest dreams, I never imagined having servants to care for me. Who cares if it's just for a couple of days.

Nina took the girls downstairs. They walked along the wide, long corridor that led to the patio.

The waiting table looked like a buffet. Baskets overflowed with all types of bread, the fresh aroma of grilled bacon wafted over everything, and hot scrambled eggs glowed beneath glass domes. Homemade peach, strawberry, and orange preserves jiggled in small silver bowls. Slices of freshly cut tropical fruits created a rainbow of colors. A pancake tower hid three different flavors—banana, chocolate chip, and blueberry. Beside it was a decanter of raw honey straight from the hive. If that wasn't enough, peaks of fresh homemade whipped cream rose from a large glass bowl. Freshly squeezed orange juice and a piping hot pot of freshly brewed coffee completed the feast.

Nina savored the meal, but Lilly and Gina ate quickly. Both were eager to jump into the pool. Nina was able to send them out on their own. In his infinite kindness, Carlo called a young swimming instructor, Elena, to observe and teach the children the correct way to stay afloat in the big pool.

Elena waited along the edge of the pool. Her dark hair was clipped behind her head. She smiled at the sight of her new pupils in their pretty swimsuits. "Aren't you two the most adorable?"

Lilly and Gina smiled politely, but shyly in response.

Elena continued to make conversation in shaky Italian. She looked at little Gina. "What's your name, sweetie?"

Gina glanced at her sister before answering confidently. "Aurora."

Lilly covered her mouth to hide that she was laughing.

Elena noticed, but she didn't think much of the girl's giggles.

* * *

Meanwhile, the adults had moved from the patio into the house's interior.

Anna excused herself to get something from her suitcase, and Nina found herself alone in the kitchen with Carlo. Moved by all the old man's kindness, she decided to open up to him. What harm could he do that was worse than what her husband had done?

"Señor Carlos," Nina said, fingers twisting around a towel hanging from the kitchen's island. "I want to tell you something more about myself."

Carlo smiled, trying to make Nina feel at ease. "Okay, but first, you have to stop calling me Señor Carlos. I know I'm old enough to be your father, but please call me Carlo. It makes me feel like we're related. Only my staff calls me *señor*, and it's not because I ask."

Nina nodded. Though she still didn't offer any names, she explained to the old man the true reason for her voyage. Carlo's kind eyes put her at ease, and she found herself opening up even further, admitting a truth she'd been reluctant to confront.

"I know I put the kids in jeopardy by bringing them on this cruise. But I had no other choice. If I came alone, it would be easy for my husband to reject me. With our children in front of him, I believe it would be more difficult." Tears rose to Nina's eyes, blinding her sight as she choked out the painful truth. "I don't care how I get him back."

Then, Nina could say no more. She broke down sobbing like a baby when their toy is taken.

Carlo sat at the kitchen island and listened throughout Nina's story. When she'd finished, he stood and began to pace the floor. The old man's brow furrowed in anger. His heart broke for her.

"I was desperate, Signore Carlo," Nina choked out, mistaking his response for one of judgment. "Please, believe me. You don't know how difficult it has been for me in the last three years without a husband."

"But I do know," Carlo said, slamming his fist on the edge of his counter. "I, of all people, know what it feels like to have your spouse taken from you! I also understand my situation was God's will, not mine. My wife was sick and her death was inevitable. But you, my sweet girl, God did not take your husband from you."

Nina looked up, blinking the tears from her eyes.

"Who is the *puta* that took your husband? She has to know that he's a married man with three children. What kind of a lowlife is he?" Carlo continued, rage making his voice tremble. "When he made those three children, he wanted to be a husband but couldn't be man enough to sustain a happy marriage? This has happened plenty of times. These lowlifes run off to America. It's the easy way out—same story, every time. First, they convince their wife they'll make more money. Then, in a few months, maybe sooner, the money stops and so do the letters and telephone calls."

Nina wiped her cheeks. Her tears were no longer from fear or sadness. She was moved by Carlo's anger.

"I know too many of these stories," the old man said, letting out a deep sigh. He stopped pacing. "The same thing happened to my niece. Thank God, I had friends in Germany where I set her up in a beautiful little home. Later, she met a fine quality man, a sports medicine physician. They have four children now and live comfortably and happily."

A loud scream from the foyer interrupted their conversation.

Nina jumped to her feet. She followed Carlo as he moved toward the foyer.

They heard Felipe's shouts before they arrived. "La Signora! La Signora Anna has fallen. Help! Someone call an ambulance!"

Anna lay on the floor near the stairs. She'd missed a step midway and tumbled down the rest. Bruises were already appearing on her limbs, and her ankle swelled like a balloon.

"*Dio mio!*" Carlo rushed to his sister. He was almost in tears. "What happened? Are you hurt?"

Nina took control of the situation. "It's okay. You're going to be alright, Signora Anna," she assured her. "Look, no blood. Can you move your legs?"

Anna tried. "Yes."

"Could you stand if I help you?"

"I'll try."

With some effort, Nina helped Anna to her feet. The old woman couldn't put weight on her right leg, but she wasn't as badly injured as her brother had feared.

Carlo watched Nina, a look of admiration on her face. He was impressed with how she'd taken control, kept her cool, and reassured Anna throughout.

You don't learn that, he thought. *It's a quality you're born with.*

By the time they got Anna to the door, the car was already waiting to take her to the hospital. Nina offered to accompany her.

"Please don't worry," she assured Carlo again. "Anna will be fine. Can you watch out for my children while I'm gone? They're still in the pool with the instructor."

Nina climbed into the front seat, but she continued to reassure Signora Anna throughout the ride. "Thank God you weren't hurt more than you were. I think God spared you."

Poor Anna, now in pain, whispered, "From your lips to God's ears."

* * *

It wasn't long after this that Nick and Carmen walked into the house.

Carlo, still visibly upset, explained what had occurred.

Concerned, Nick and Carmen offered to go to the hospital. They wanted to help in some way.

"Thank you, but that's not necessary," Carlo assured them. "I'd rather you both stay here and help me with the children. They're in the pool."

"Of course!" Nick agreed. "Come on, let's go outside. At least we're all together in good company. Your sister will be taken care of and return better than fine."

He continued to reassure his godfather as they went to the pool.

It was then that Nick saw his daughters.

Lilly and Gina played in the pool with their new instructor. They wore their new swimsuits, swim caps and goggles.

Nick didn't recognize them.

The girls didn't recognize him either.

It had been over three years since Nick left Sicily. Lilly had been only two years old, and Gina barely two months. They had no memories of their father's face. He had no idea how they now looked.

Elena introduced the girls to them as Bianca and Aurora.

Already in their swimsuits, Nick and Carmen joined them in the pool.

Very quickly, Nick took a liking to the unfamiliar children. He began playing with them, splashing them and tossing them into the water.

When it was time for lunch, they climbed from the pool and walked to the covered veranda where it would be served. Lilly rode on Nick's shoulders. Gina stood on his feet, her hands lifted and wrapped around his fingers for support. One of Nick's flip-flops slipped off. The girls laughed about it all the way to the veranda. He joined them, finding their giggles infectious.

Nick fixed their plates. He made sure they ate.

It never crossed Nick's mind that they were his own flesh and blood.

* * *

Nick spotted Carlo approaching. Leaving the girls with Carmen and Elena, he ran over to his godfather. "Have you heard anything from the hospital? How is your sister?"

"Good news and bad. My sister is okay, no internal bruising or damage, but she has a bad sprain with torn tissues in her ankle. She has to stay on complete bed rest for at least two days. Thank goodness, for her sweet, young companion. She's been with her the entire time at the hospital." Carlo pressed his hand to his heart. "I want to make this up to her. I promised myself that."

"Isn't your warm and generous hospitality enough?" Nick suggested.

"No, this girl needs my help. Can you imagine such a sweet woman with a deadbeat husband? I mean, a real scum. I would like to meet him someday. I could make his life so miserable he'd wish he wasn't born on this planet."

"Wow, it's that bad, huh?" Nick patted his godfather's shoulder. "Come on, cheer up. The kids are waiting for us."

They walked toward the veranda.

"What time do you expect them back from the hospital?" Nick asked. "Should we wait for them to eat?"

"No, it's okay. They're doing further tests. Anna hit her head numerous times on the granite when she fell down the stairs. I'm surprised there wasn't blood everywhere. Thank God."

Chapter Twelve

Despite his worries about his sister, Carlo decided to make the best of the remaining day. He enjoyed the company of Nick, Carmen, and the two little girls.

They rode horses, had a picnic, and played games. Throughout the day, Carlo beamed in pride at the sight of his godson.

He's so good with those girls, the old man thought. *They just love him!*

After dinner, Lucia and Paloma took the children to get ready for bed. Nick and Carmen remained at the dining table with Carlo.

"Are you comfortable in the villa?" the old man asked, preparing to retire for the night as well. "Do you need anything else?"

Nick shook his head. "We have more than what anyone could ask for."

"You're spoiling us," Carmen agreed. "I think I may want to live here forever."

She was only joking, but Carlo's response was serious.

"Say the word and the beach house is yours. Nick is my relative, even if it's not by blood. I've always treated him as if he was one of my own sons. If he wants, he can move here. I'll give him a job overseeing my assets and managing my staff. It'll come with a house, a new car, and a very generous salary. He can set his own hours. There'll be no hard labor, no mixing cement or building houses."

Nick and Carmen exchanged a look. Both were thinking the same thing: How could anyone refuse such an offer?

* * *

That night at the beach house, Carmen snuggled against Nick on the couch.

"Was he serious about having you move here?" Carmen asked. "You *and* me, obviously. I'm sure I was included." She laughed.

"I don't know."

"Screw you, Nicholas." Carmen pushed away from him. "You're not moving anywhere without me."

Nick grinned. "Why, if I didn't know better, I'd think you really love me."

"Who's talking about *you*? I'm in love with this whole lifestyle." Carmen spread her arms out at the luxury surrounding them before collapsing into the cushions. She winked to let him know she was only teasing.

Nick laughed and stood. "You want a drink?"

"As long as it's not sangria."

He went to the kitchen and returned with two ice-cold beers and a bag of chips for them to share.

"So what are we doing tomorrow?" Carmen asked.

"I don't care, whatever you want."

"We still have those day-cruise vouchers we purchased at the airport," Carmen suggested. "Then maybe a nice dinner afterwards? Just the two of us."

"Sure." Nick shrugged. "Once everything is okay with Carlo's sister. I'll call him in the morning to check in. If he doesn't need us for anything, we'll go."

* * *

Early the next morning, Nick called the house. Felipe answered with his usual greeting before getting Carlo on the phone.

"How's Anna?" Nick asked.

"She's doing well. They came home this morning around five. She didn't want to stay at the hospital any longer and was threatening to sign herself out. Is she my sister or what? Just like me, very demanding!"

Both men shared a laugh.

Happy to hear that Anna was well, Nick broached the topic of the day cruise.

Carlo agreed at once. "Are you kidding? Take your Signorina Caramella on this cruise. I feel bad you had to stay in yesterday and babysit."

"If there was any babysitting, I was the baby," Nick assured him. "The way you spoil me and Carmen? I could never thank you enough. And those kids were a pleasure to be around. I had a great time with them!"

"My dear godson, one day you'll be the most amazing father," Carlo said. He had no idea how ironic his statement was, especially in the context. "The girl who marries you will be a lucky woman! Personally, I hope it'll be Caramella—I adore her—but it's your choice."

Nick, who could make no promises when it came to marriage, chuckled politely on the other end.

"Go, have the best time!" Carlo repeated. "Enjoy your cruise. I'll send a car to take you and collect you. Give him the name of the cruise company and he'll find out what time you're returning."

"Thank you, Godfather. Thank you for all you do for us. See you tomorrow."

Chapter Thirteen

Luca drove Nick and Carmen to the San Juan marina, where all the cruise ships lined the dock. People crowded the area. Hoping for a more private experience with Carmen, Nick paid for an upgrade on The Star of San Juan. For ten hours, the yacht and its crew would be theirs to command. Nick and Carmen would be the only passengers. They could choose which islands to visit and how long to stay.

The Star of San Juan was clean and in excellent condition. Captain George Torres welcomed them aboard. The first mate and cook, Diego, offered them tall glasses of cocktails. Even though it was only a day trip, other crew carried their bags to the private quarters below.

With Nick's approval, Captain George planned the day's itinerary, and soon they were off.

Nick and Carmen climbed down the steps. They looked at the large bedroom with an attached bathroom and shower, a sitting area with a mahogany bar, and a pool table.

"Wow, can you believe this?" said Carmen.

"It's special," Nick replied.

They changed into their swimwear. Nick was faster. He returned to the top deck first. There was a curved Italian white leather sofa that could seat eight near the front of the boat. Holding onto the side of ship's rails, he made his way forward.

Carmen arrived on deck a few minutes. Nick was all smiles.

Though they had been advised to wear wet shirts to avoid getting sunburned, Carmen in typical fashion ignored the warning. She changed into a blue-and-white two-piece bathing suit with a matching silk sarong. Rows of ruffles flowed at the bottom, swaying in the warm breeze as she crossed the deck.

Nick wrapped her in his arms the minute she was on the couch.

They passed by the landmarks of Puerto Rico. Captain George explained the history behind each one.

The [Castillo San Felipe del Morro](#) was the most recognizable and historically significant landmark in Puerto Rico. *Nacimiento del Nuevo Mundo*, the island's tallest statue, was known as *La Estatua de Colón*. It was a 360-foot bronze sculpture located on the Atlantic coastline of Arecibo. Then, there was the Cabo Rojo Lighthouse.

Later, after the sightseeing was finished, Nick and Carmen settled on the wooden deck, spreading out their towels to soak up the sun.

Diego emerged with a six-foot charcuterie board, and a bucket filled with ice and bottles of champagne, white wine and sparkling Moscato. He rested the food on a large round butcher-block table.

The board was filled with mini sandwiches, four types of cheeses—tropical *queso cremita, queso de papa*, a wheel of creamy French Brie, and a large wedge of good old Italian Parmigiano—salami, prosciutto, guava and cheese *pastelitos*, nuts, chips, and an assortment of sliced papaya, avocado, dragon fruit, mango, and pineapple.

The meal had a satisfying savory taste, complemented by the drinks. It was delightful.

Captain George informed them that they would soon arrive at Isla Palominos, a small uninhabited island located about a mile east of Puerto Rico.

"It's a private a hundred-acre getaway with pristine white beaches, available exclusively to resort guests and high-profile, wealthy individuals," the captain explained. "While there, you can have fun at El Conquistador's Coqui Water Park, where you can experience two-hundred-and-fifty-three feet of speed thrills and sensational splashes with a heart-pounding speed slide and a massive vertical drop. There is also a lazy river and an expansive infinity edge pool overlooking the sea."

Nick was impressed. If the private cruise gave them access to this island, it had been worth the price.

"If you guys are interested in golf," the captain continued, "there is an eighteen-hole golf course."

Carmen giggled and poked Nick's side. "The only sport he likes is *bocce*."

The captain understood and smiled. "There's food all over the island for free—barbecue stations with the best seafood, fresh fruit from the island, and of course, an open bar all day and night wherever you go. It's all-inclusive."

The first thing Carmen wanted to do was snorkel and see the coral reefs. "If I see a piece that I like, we'll have the jeweler from Cabo Rojo set it in a bracelet or necklace. I definitely want the Tiffany Blue stone."

Two jet skis picked them up and carried them to an enchanted area where they could snorkel. It was a heavenly delight. Coral of every color, shape, and size glistened beneath the waves. Carmen took more than she could carry, slipping some into the pockets of Nick's swimsuit.

"Are you serious?" He stared at the corals she was still clutching in her hands. "You really want all of those?"

"Nah," Carmen responded in her Brooklyn accent, "but a girl's gotta choose."

"Unloosen your bathing suit. I think it's too tight and you're not getting circulation to your brain."

"Lighten up." Carmen swatted him with her elbow, kicking to stay afloat. "I'm just going to buy two of them."

"Ok, get out of the water before you see something else you like."

"But I do see something else I like." Carmen let out one of her famous giggles, reeling Nick in. "I see your hairy legs and something further up—those I want before the stones."

Her teasing made Nick's heart melt.

"Did you put on sunscreen?" Carmen asked. Both of them had turned beet red from the sun.

"Only on my private parts."

"Thank goodness. Wouldn't want my friends to get sunburned. What time did you tell Carlo we would be back?"

"I didn't tell him a time. But Carmelo knows we're going to dinner at El Delfin Blanco after this. Hopefully he'll have told my godfather, so he knows not to wait on us to eat."

"Oh good," Carmen said, but her mind was already elsewhere. "You know, it must be a lot of fun driving your own jet ski on the water. Let's do that next."

"Don't you want to go to that Coqui Water Park?"

Carmen pouted like a little girl. "Just an hour of jet skis. Come on, please?"

How could he refuse her?

Nick and Carmen were having so much fun that they both didn't want the day to end, but it did. Everything would now be just a beautiful memory.

* * *

Carmelo collected them from their dinner at El Delfin Blanco and drove them back to the Castillo.

Carlo greeted them when they arrived.

"*Nick, figlio affezionato mio*! Did you enjoy the day? And you, my little *Caramella*, did my godson spoil you?"

"He always does," Carmen answered first. "But today he was the prince of all princes."

"*Fantastico!* It makes my heart very happy."

"It was an amazing day," Nick agreed. "I learned so much about Puerto Rico, its heritage, the story, and how proud the people are of their magnificent island. Plus, it's very beautiful, and you still have land here that is uninhabited, whereas in the U.S., most of the land is used for crops or someone lives there."

"Wonderful, wonderful!" Carlo walked with them through the house. There were no sounds of conversation from out on the patio.

"Where is everyone?" Nick asked. He'd expected to find Carlo's sister and her friend still awake and enjoying their night on the patio.

"They hardly slept last night," Carlo explained. "They retired early."

"I'm sorry I missed them. I wanted to meet your sister and the children's mother."

"What time is your flight tomorrow?"

"Eight-thirty in the morning," Nick said. "I want to get there at least an hour and a half before."

Carlo sighed. "Then this is goodbye."

"Not for good. I know where you live now. I promise you I'll visit so often, you'll get tired of me."

"Test me."

Nick laughed. "Come on, *parrinu*. You know I keep my word, especially with you."

The two embraced in a long hug. Then, Carlo took Nick's head in his hands and stared straight into his eyes. "I'll be waiting for you, my son."

Nick was almost moved to tears. Before he could grow too emotional, however, Carmen interrupted. She embraced Carlo and promised that they would return soon.

As they walked out the door, Felipe approached. He saw tears glistening in the corners of Carlo's eyes. "Padron, you love that guy, don't you?"

"I do," he said.

Chapter Fourteen

As he was wiping his tears, Nina came down from upstairs. "Is everything alright, Signore Carlo?"

"Everything is just fine, my dear," Carlo assured her. "Like a fruit that ripens with sunshine, this old man gets more sentimental with age."

Nina had come down looking for cough syrup for one of the girls. Felipe went to fetch it. Nina sat in the dining room and talked with Carlo in the meantime.

"The man that just left is my godson," Carlo explained. "I knew the family for many years, even before I ventured to America."

"You baptized him when you were still in Sicily? That's nice that you kept in touch."

"But we didn't," Carlo said. "He heard I'd moved to Puerto Rico and managed to get my number. You can't believe how happy I was to hear his voice on the phone!"

"Where does he live?"

"Somewhere in New York."

What a coincidence! Nina thought. "That's where I'm going after I dock in Miami. Hopefully, immigration will give me a visa to enter the U.S."

"So you're going to find your husband there?"

"Yes."

"I hope you find him."

"My children need him. And may I be totally honest with you, Signore Carlo? After all he's put me through, I still love and worry about him."

"You're a good woman. Your parents taught you well. Nowadays, the smallest fight between a husband and wife, and they need therapy and a divorce. There's always an argument in a marriage, but you learn from them and move forward. The marriage gets stronger because you learned from the battles."

"That makes sense," she said.

He wasn't finished yet. "It's like a new driver—if he never gets lost, he will never know which is the wrong road."

"You have so much wisdom, Signore Carlo," Nina said. "A man who finds wisdom gains understanding. You, Signore Carlo, are very understanding."

"It's the experience in life you go through," Carlo agreed. As they were having this pleasant conversation, the doorbell rang.

With a bewildered look, Carlo asked, "Who could that be at this hour?"

They heard muffled chat in the foyer but couldn't make out who it was. Then the front door closed.

Soon Felipe entered the dining room. "It was your godson, *señor*. His girl had forgotten her backpack on the chair. I gave it to him, and he left."

"Had I known it was him, I would have asked him to come in for a minute and meet you," Carlo said to Nina. "My godson is also from the old school, a gem of a guy. He's got this girl who is his equal; they will stay together for a hundred years. I'm sure of it!"

"What's his name?" Nina asked.

"Nick. His name is Nick."

That did not raise a red flag at all.

Nina had never heard such a name. Nick was English. She'd only ever called her husband *Nicola*, the Italian version.

Felipe brought the cough syrup.

Nina took it and retreated for the night, no idea how close she'd just been to seeing the very man she'd left Sicily to find.

* * *

Destiny played a major part during that trip. Nick and Nina had found themselves not only on the same island, but in the same home. Yet, their meeting was not to be.

Not yet.

Nick and Carmen departed early the next morning. They were already in the air before the others sat at the table for a late breakfast.

Carlo was like a puppy dog, sad and quiet. He'd lost his beloved godson, and his sister and Nina were leaving to Miami. Their cruise departed later that afternoon. Soon, the old man would be alone again.

Breakfast was served outside on the covered veranda, and Carlo ate without tasting his meal. His eyes moved from Nina to her daughters. He'd grown so fond of all three of them.

After the meal, as the housekeepers helped Anna back upstairs to pack, Carlo took Nina to the kitchen for a private chat.

"I have an idea," he said.

"What is it?" said Nina, curious.

"If you get through in Miami, you'll be able to take a flight to New York without a problem. Call and give me the flight information if you manage. I'll ask Nick to pick you up from the airport. I know he'll do me this favor."

Nina couldn't believe it. She was so overjoyed.

"You're a godsend, Signore Carlo. How can I ever repay you?"

"You know how you can repay me? By finding your husband and being happy. That's what I want for you. And then one day, come down here with him."

* * *

Luca carried their luggage to the car that afternoon.

Nina's eyes filled with tears as she watched. The time had come to say goodbye. It was harder than they'd all expected.

Lilly and Gina had their arms around Carlo's neck. They wouldn't let go, nor did the old man want them to.

Despite her injured ankle, Signora Anna was the strong one. Holding back tears, she kissed her brother's cheeks and told him, "Take good care of yourself, *mi senti?*"

Luca helped her into the car, then helped to pry the children from Carlo.

Nina was the last to say goodbye. She embraced the old man. "*Grazie. Grazie* a million times for all you've done for me."

"You don't need to thank me. I did it from my heart because I felt it."

As Nina walked to the car, she turned to look at him, thinking it would be the last time. "I love you, Signore Carlo. You made me feel I had a father here."

Tears streamed from the old man's face as he watched them leave.

Chapter Fifteen

Anna and Nina boarded the cruise ship ahead of schedule. Lunch was being served, but after their late breakfast, none of them were hungry.

Instead, Signora Anna accompanied Nina to her cabin. They sat and talked about the *castillo*, the undeniable hospitality and warmth Nina had received, and the love they shared for Carlo.

"Just talking about him fills my heart with such admiration. Thank you, Signora Anna, for giving me the honor of meeting your brother," Nina said. "If I had to describe the characteristics of a good man, I would say that your brother surpasses all of them. He has a great personality and a heart of gold. He listens more than he talks, takes initiative, has plenty of friends, and has a great relationship with people he knows. I also noticed in him a balance of empathy and gratitude, and most of all, he always has a smile on his face and love in his heart."

"Oh, Nina, such beautiful words for my brother," replied Anna.

"And if I may say so, you are the female version of him."

"Now you're going to make me cry," said Signora Anna. Feeling emotionally overcome and tired from their travels, she then suggested. "Let's all take a quick nap, and we'll meet in the dining room for dinner."

"Yes, Signora Anna, if I haven't said it enough, thank you. Thank you for being my best friend, mother, and sister." She wrapped the older woman in a hug.

Heart swelling with joy, Anna walked out of Nina's cabin.

* * *

At six-thirty, Anna was already sitting at the table in the dining room. She waited for them and soon saw the children run to her.

"My little munchkins, I couldn't wait to see you. How beautiful you both look!"

In gratitude, Nina said, "It's all the gifts and clothing that your brother purchased for them. He sent us home with even more gift boxes. We opened some earlier and felt like it was Christmas. Just the Santa and the tree were missing."

Little Gina tugged on Anna's sleeve. "And all of our toys and dolls were there! Even the tea sets."

"I expect to be invited to the tea party with all your dolls," Anna said.

"That's a great idea!" Gina clapped her hands.

Seeing her daughter's excitement warmed Nina's heart. But she couldn't shake her fear. Tomorrow, they landed in Miami. She'd have to face U.S. immigration.

What if this was the calm before the storm?

* * *

The following morning, Nina's fate was decided.

She woke early after a restless night and hurried to the shower. It was the only place she could cry without her daughters seeing.

The second she stepped out of the bathroom, the children awoke complaining that they wanted food. Nina bathed them quickly before taking them to the dining room.

To her surprise, Signora Anna was already there, sipping a cup of coffee.

"Why are you here so early?" Nina asked.

Wet lines streaked Signora Anna's face. She'd been crying as well.

Anna patted her cheeks.

"Why the tears?" Nina asked.

The older woman couldn't find the words to explain. Her mouth quivered from trying not to cry. After a moment, everything she'd bottled up came pouring from her.

"You've been on my mind all night. I have a heart, and I feel for you. Nick doesn't deserve you, my sweet friend. You deserve someone much better than your husband. I know you still love him. I can tell by the way you speak of him. I'm sorry if I'm out of line, but it hurts me to see you this way. Not knowing what the outcome will be just kills me."

The old woman closed her eyes, holding back tears. Nina was touched by her concern. But Signora Anna wasn't finished.

"Listen—I have an apartment in New York all set up, thanks to my brother. If you need someplace to stay, please do not hesitate. You are more than welcome to stay with me."

The older woman took a deep breath, keeping her voice low, and trying to speak so that the girls wouldn't hear from the opposite end of the table.

"But first, let's see what happens in Miami. I'll be by your side the entire time. We'll present ourselves together with all the passports and paperwork. Maybe, by some luck, the agent will get confused."

Nina couldn't believe it. She'd met an angel on her cruise ship.

"How can I ever repay you for what you're offering?" Nina whispered, trying to hide her tears from her children. Then another fact occurred to her. The old woman would see her daughters' names on the passports. "And this whole time, I haven't been honest with you, or your brother."

"What's this?" Signora Anna's eyebrows rose. Another person might've been quick to assume the worst and scold Nina, but Anna trusted her instincts. She'd seen something genuine in the young woman before her and wouldn't leap to conclusions.

"The girls aren't really named Bianca and Aurora."

"Ah. That." Signora Anna smiled. "The Disney princesses. I suspected as much."

"You did?" Nina couldn't believe it. She'd thought the ruse so clever that she'd been afraid to come clean.

"Carlo and I discussed it, but we didn't want to pry. What are their names?"

"Lilly and Gina." It felt good to say the names aloud again. Tears welled in Nina's eyes. She couldn't believe that the older woman wasn't upset with her. "You truly are a saint, Signora Anna. I don't deserve your kindness."

"Of course, you do." Signora Anna patted her hand. "*Andiamo.* The line will be endless if we don't move fast."

They left the dining room. Both Lilly and Gina carried croissants, still eating. With crumbs dropping onto the floor, they took the elevator to the mezzanine level and walked to the baggage claim area.

Suitcases spun around on conveyor belts. Signora Anna found hers first. With a struggle, Nina managed to grab one of her bags. However, her other two were missing.

Nina felt relieved by the momentary dilemma. It meant more time before she would face the immigration officer.

"Signora Anna, stay here with the kids. You must be tired of walking," Nina said, as they walked through the conveyor belts. "How is your foot?"

"It's fine, no need to worry about me."

"I'll go look at the conveyor belt. If they're not there, I'll know where to look. A woman on the ship mentioned to me that sometimes, if the conveyor belt is full, the workers pull some luggage off and set it against the wall."

Sure enough, the other two pieces of luggage were at the far end against the wall. Nina grabbed both and brought them to Signora Anna.

There was nothing left to do. Suitcases in tow, they continued. Nina's heart pounded in her chest.

This was the moment she'd dreaded the entire trip. Nina was about to find out if she could get a visa.

* * *

The immigration line was long, but it moved quickly. In a matter of minutes, they were face-to-face with an immigration agent. The tone of his voice expressed his authority.

"Please pass me your disembarkation slip, your declaration papers, and your passports," he commanded.

Anna put all the passports and papers in front of him.

"Are you all from the Transatlantic Cruise ship?" he asked.

Nina was too afraid to speak. Anna answered. "Yes."

The immigration officer considered the passports one at a time. There were three in total. Due to her age, Gina shared one with her mother. However, her information appeared on a different page.

He opened Signora Anna's first and stamped her visa. Accepted.

Next, he looked at Lilly's passport. He stapled card with a temporary thirty-day visa beside her picture.

Then, the officer came to Nina's passport.

When her name was processed in the computer, the word *denied* appeared in bold red letters.

He couldn't give her a visa.

However, Gina was another matter. She was only a child. Nothing came up in the system for her. He stamped a paper with a thirty-day visa for the little girl, then stapled it into the passport.

But the officer made a mistake.

Amid the confusion of the many disembarkation slips, declaration papers, and passports, he stapled the visa paper onto Nina's page. On Gina's, he placed the card that said *denied*.

Nina caught the mistake at once. The moment she was out of the officer's sight, she pulled the *denied* index card from the passport. She didn't want to give anyone reason to check the details of the visa on her page. Otherwise, they'd realize it was for a child and not for an adult woman.

Nina watched Gina running loose around the immigration area, playing a game of her own, slipping through rows of luggage. No one noticed.

They exited the immigration area. Another officer waited at the exit gate to double-check the passports.

He never looked at the date of birth.

Instead, he assumed the two visa permits were for a mother and her daughter. Little Gina was in the luggage cart, getting a free ride. No one spotted or questioned her.

All walked out without a problem.

And, just like that, Nina was on U.S. soil.

Chapter Sixteen

Nina burst into tears and hugged Signora Anna. To anyone watching, it looked like a mother and daughter reuniting in tears.

The first thing they did was call Carlo and inform him of Nina's luck.

When Anna finished the story, the old man was ecstatic. "I'm so glad everything worked out. She's been on my mind since you ladies left here."

"I'm going to bring Nina with me to the apartment in New York tonight," Anna informed him. "I couldn't just abandon her at a hotel alone. Tomorrow morning, she'll start looking for that dog of a husband, and we'll see how he handles the news that his wife has come to America. I'm worried he might refuse her calls, or worse."

"You are an angel, my loving sister, and God will repay you in good will," Carlo exclaimed. "If you need money, don't hesitate to tell me. I know you are a proud woman. I've already decided that I'm going to have my accountant give you a check for ten thousand dollars to use for yourself, Nina, and the little girls. Buy her whatever she needs. Those kids didn't look like they had much when they were here."

Anna pressed her hand to her chest, moved by her brother's generosity.

Before she could thank him, Carlo continued. "Listen to me carefully. I need to know who this bastard is. Nina never told me his name, just to protect him."

"Carlo, she never told me his name either. I don't know who he is, but he's from our neck of the woods."

"Find out his name. Then, we'll take care of this. Did you book a flight to New York?"

"No, not yet," Anna said. "Nina insisted we call you first."

"Ah! Such a sweet girl!" Carlo said. "I'm glad you both have each other. How is your foot? I want you to take care of yourself, you hear me? Try to stay off of it as much as you can and call me the minute you get to the apartment."

Anna finally got the chance to thank him. No amount of gratitude felt sufficient. She ended the call with a reminder of how much she loved him. "*Sangu mio, ti voglio bene, frate mio.*"

"*Puru io sangu mio.*" He echoed the sentiment, and they hung up.

*　*　*

Anna booked them four one-way tickets to New York. Then the four of them took a cab to Miami International Airport.

Nina stared out the window in amazement. Everything was so different from her hometown in Sicily.

Skyscrapers loomed over the streets. Cars, packed bumper-to-bumper, lined the massive roads. People rollerbladed past on the sidewalks. There were so many bikes!

What really caught Nina's attention was the clothing. People wore shorts and summer clothes with flip-flops. She'd heard about the temperature in New York. It hadn't occurred to her that Florida would be different.

How big is America to have different climates in different cities? she wondered.

Her eyes grew wide, trying to see everything: the large roads, the greenery in the middle of the streets. The swaying palms made her feel like she was in a dream. Everything was new and clean. Even the heavy traffic felt ordered, everyone obeying and respecting the traffic laws. In

Italy, the *parking lot* was wherever there was space. People would cut through your living room if it would help them pass another car.

Nina was just as mesmerized when they arrived at the airport.

Everything in the airport was new construction: gift shops, restaurants, lounges. Comfortable, wide leather chairs ran throughout the concourses.

Holding Gina in her arms, Nina stepped onto a motorized walkway. She tried not to look amazed.

"What will they think of next?" she said.

Anna smiled. "I'll tell you one thing. In this airport, they have sleeping pods you can rent by the hour. It's to accommodate travelers who have connecting flights with long layovers."

"Well then, if he doesn't want us, maybe we can rent one of these pods to sleep in."

"That's not even funny, Nina."

* * *

Soon, the four of them were seated on the aircraft. Lilly sat by the window. Gina took the center, and Nina got the aisle. Signora Anna sat across from her, in the same row but on the other half of the plane. They all settled in and buckled their seatbelts.

The captain's voice boomed from the loudspeaker. "Welcome on board American Airlines, flight number two-seventy-one to New York City."

He'd spoken in English. Nina didn't understand a word. But the calm expression on Signora Anna's face told her not to panic.

The plane rolled down the runway and soon they were in the sky.

Lilly pressed her face to the window. Gina leaned over, trying to see outside as well.

"Mamma," Lilly asked. "Are we in heaven? Because there are only clouds up here."

"No, my precious girl. We're in a plane over the clouds," Nina explained.

The sky was dark most of the flight. Then, New York City came into view. The girls gasped.

"Doesn't this look like the nativity Nonna sets up each Christmas?" Nina asked. "All colorful tiny lights in the darkness."

"Is it Christmas here, Mama?" Gina asked.

"No, baby, their Christmas is the same time as ours. The lights you see are from the big city."

* * *

They arrived on schedule. There was no immigration or customs agent to face this time. All they had to do was get their suitcases, and soon they were on their way to Signora Anna's apartment.

It was located in an upscale neighborhood in uptown Manhattan. The building had a doorman, and the apartment had a balcony overlooking Central Park.

Originally, the place had belonged to Carlo, who'd lived in the apartment with his wife before moving to Puerto Rico. However, he'd signed it over permanently to his sister, so she'd have a home of her own when she returned to the city.

It had been a while since Anna visited. But the doorman, George, recognized her when they arrived.

He greeted her with a warm welcome. "My dear Signora Anna, how are you? It's so good to see you! And how is your brother? Is he here too?"

"It's great to see you too, George. No, Carlo isn't here. He's much too busy in Puerto Rico, but who knows? Maybe he'll surprise me and come stay with me while I'm here."

"Oh, Signora, that would give me so much pleasure to see him again," said George. "I was so sorry to hear of the passing of his beloved wife, your sister-in-law."

Signora Anna, in her soft speaking tone, said, "Thank you, George."

With that, the bellboy retrieved the suitcases and carry-ons from the car and carried them up to the apartment. Nina and the girls followed.

Signora Anna's apartment was on the top floor of the building. It was the penthouse suite, and she had her own private foyer.

When the elevator dinged to a stop, there was only one door before them. Signora Anna led them through.

Once again, Nina was in awe. She felt like her children, staring at the clouds and the city lights.

"Signora Anna, I might well get used to all of this," Nina said, unable to hold back her smile. She wrapped her arms around the older woman. "Bless your heart. You're a good woman just like your brother, and God sees all you do. Do I need to tell you that both of you are so deserving of all you have?"

"Oh Nina, I am grateful, and I do thank the Lord every day for all I have. But my brother is not all that grateful. After losing his beautiful Giovanna, he once told me, *I'd rather be poor and have my wife still here with me than be rich and powerful and not have her to share it with.* Money is not all that matters in life."

You can say those things after you have money, but can you say it when you're dirt poor? Nina kept the thought to herself.

"Come, let me show you the rooms," Anna said.

She led Nina to the kitchen, all in white with a tint of gray. A massive island with six stools around it stood in the center.

"For breakfast and lunch," Anna explained.

A built-in private elevator carried them upstairs to the bedroom. Carlo had installed it for his wife when they lived in the apartment.

Nina was given a room to herself. The girls had one to share with twin beds. The rooms had a jack and jill bathroom between them.

"I'll get lost in a bed so big!" Nina insisted. "Honestly, we could all share my room. It could easily fit all three of us, and having the girls in my bed will stop my thoughts from wandering to him."

"You're welcome to share if that's what you truly wish," Anna assured her. Thinking the family might want some time alone, the older woman made to retreat. However, Nina and the girls followed her back downstairs to continue the tour.

The pantry was filled with food, and so was the refrigerator—milk, eggs, bread, juices, and all the essentials had been purchased prior to Anna's arrival.

The girls sat around the island. Nina made them grilled cheese sandwiches, an American classic. They loved them.

Anna found a restaurant still open for delivery and placed an order for herself. However, Nina insisted she was as satisfied with a cheese sandwich as her children.

By the time the older woman's food arrived, the girls were getting sleepy. Nina went upstairs to put them to bed.

Signora Anna finished her meal, then sat on a soft leather club chair out on the enclosed balcony, which overlooked Central Park. It was her favorite part of the apartment. She called her brother one last time.

"I'm sorry," Carlo said. "I couldn't get hold of Nick to pick up you guys from the airport."

"It's okay, Carlo. We took a cab."

"Did you find out his name from Nina, yet?"

Anna yawned. "Not yet."

"Hopefully you can get it. I've reached out to a private investigator, but Nick knows a lot more people from our neck of the woods up there in New York. I want to give him this dog's name. Maybe Nick can track him down."

Carlo had no idea that, when he called his beloved godson, he'd be talking to the very dog he was trying to catch.

Chapter Seventeen

Early the next morning, Nina awoke with her heart fluttering. Her daughters, however, were full of excitement. They leaped out of bed, thrilled to be in New York, and rushed to the elevator.

Nina's heart relaxed at the sight of her children playing happily. She felt nothing but happiness for her children as she went downstairs into the kitchen.

Signora Anna sat by the large island in the kitchen. With a big smile, the older woman spread her arms in greeting. "*Buon giorno*, Nina. How did you sleep?"

"Like a baby in her mother's arms," Nina said, pulling out a stool to join Anna.

"Would you like an espresso or a cappuccino?" Anna offered.

"Whatever is easier," Nina said politely. "I don't want to bother you more than I already have."

"Don't be silly! You're no bother to me. Just the opposite. Don't forget, I live here alone, so I welcome good company." Anna stood. The swelling in her ankle had gone down, and she was able to walk the few feet to the coffee machine without issue. "So, what's next, Nina? How do we start this search for your husband? Personally, I think you should forget him. He doesn't deserve a wonderful wife like you searching for him."

Signora Anna turned and carried a large cup of cappuccino in her hands to Nina. Then it suddenly occurred to her what she'd said.

"Please, don't get me wrong," Anna said, patting Nina's shoulder as she rested the coffee before her. "I'm old enough to be your mother, and I just want the best for you."

"I could never misinterpret your intentions, Signora Anna," Nina assured, staring at the hot cappuccino. It had been her preferred drink whenever they'd had time to sit and chat on the cruise. She smiled and took the older woman's hand. "You've been nearly a mother to me, giving me advice like only a mother could. But I can't help it. I still love him, no matter what he's put me through."

Nina sighed, casting her eyes down.

Signora Anna squeezed her hands. "It's your call, sweetie."

"I can't explain it in words," Nina said, turning toward the kitchen island. She put both hands on her cup. The white foam on top of her cappuccino reminded her of the cascading waterfall in Carlo's pool. "My heart just won't let go. Sometimes I wish it would so I could start a new life for myself and my children. That's what hurts me the most—knowing I'm setting this example for them, allowing them to think it's okay to live in a loveless marriage, to be rejected and still love the man."

Signora Anna sat. She placed a hand on Nina's arm and offered an understanding smile.

It made Nina feel safe, and she opened more of her heart to the kind older woman.

"I hate that they're seeing me in agony. But how do I fix it? Lilly already suspects something is off. The other day she asked me, *Mamma, why doesn't Daddy want to be with us? Did we do something wrong?* And I—" Nina cut off, bursting into tears. Her sobs soon became uncontrollable.

Signora Anna let her cry for a minute before patting her back.

"Okay," the older woman said, taking control of the situation. "If we have to find this man, we can't do it by sitting here and crying. Let's get to business."

Signora Anna informed Nina about her call with Carlo the previous night.

"He hired a private investigator? Just to help me?" Nina couldn't believe it.

"Yes, and the minute I hear something, I will tell you immediately."

Nina blinked back the tears, still falling down her cheeks. "How can I ever repay what you and Signore Carlo have done and continue to do for me?"

Then something occurred to Nina.

She wiped her eyes and turned to her bag, which she'd rested on the kitchen island beside her. Tucked in a hidden compartment within her wallet was a piece of paper.

Nina pulled it out and passed it to Signora Anna.

The older woman read the four lines written on the page. "Whose address is this?"

"It's his," Nina said. "Or at least, it was. Last time I heard from him, he was sharing the apartment with two other Sicilian guys. I don't have a phone number, just that address."

"So, what do you want to do? Go there?"

Nina nodded. "I want to see if he really lives there. I have no choice. I've got to find him to talk to him."

Signora Anna's heart dropped. She had a gut feeling that Nina's husband was up to no good.

What if he's living there with another woman? The same fear crossed her mind whenever her new friend spoke of her missing husband. *I pray Nina won't find them together.*

The old woman's chest felt heavy with worry. "Listen, Nina, I know you're determined to find him, but please be prepared for the worst outcome."

"What do you mean, Signora Anna?"

"I was always taught to be prepared for the worst outcome because you don't need to prepare for an outcome with a good ending."

"Oh, Signora Anna, you're worrying too much," Nina tried to reassure her. "Please, don't worry. I'll take care of myself whatever the outcome."

* * *

Now that she had the address, Signora Anna began making arrangements. She didn't know much about Brooklyn so sought advice from a close friend.

While the older woman talked on the phone, Nina waited on the balcony, holding her empty cup and staring at Central Park below. It was a magnificent sight.

"Evidently, the neighborhood is not too safe," Signora Anna informed as she joined Nina on the balcony. Her voice was laced with concern.

"I'm not going to tour the neighborhood," Nina said, smiling in an effort to relax her friend. "Please, don't be scared for me."

"Okay," she said, but the fear remained etched on her face as she took a seat beside Nina. "My nephew Matteo lives in Brooklyn. Let's see if he's available. If he is, I'll have my driver collect him so that he can accompany you to the address. But please, Nina, the minute you're back in the car, call me. You're not taking the kids, are you?"

Nina looked uncertain. "I had intended to take them with me. He might be more sympathetic with them there. He'd have to be heartless to reject me in front of his own children."

The worry grew on Signora Anna's face. She didn't like the idea of the two, sweet little girls discovering an uncomfortable truth about their father. How would they feel if their poor mother broke down? On the other hand, perhaps Nina would feel stronger with one of them there.

Still not entirely comfortable with the idea, Anna proposed Nina take only her older daughter. "The little one can stay here with me."

"Yes, that's a good idea," Nina agreed. It would be easier to manage with only one child. Plus, though Signora Anna didn't know it, Lilly could've passed as her father's clone. They had the same face, same cheeks, and same curly black hair.

Once that decision had been made, Signora Anna returned to the phone. First, she contacted her nephew. He was free, so she asked him to accompany Nina to the address and instructed him never to leave her friend alone. Then, Signora Anna made the necessary arrangements with her driver.

Ten minutes later, Nina was in a car heading to Brooklyn.

Chapter Eighteen

Signora Anna tapped her fingers nervously on the kitchen counter. Her eyes darted to the clock on the wall. It had been almost an hour since Nina left.

Little Gina played happily with her new dolls in the living room, unaware that her mother and sister had left for a dangerous part of the city to find the man who'd abandoned them. Anna envied the child's peace of mind. Her heart raced with fear for Nina. She couldn't shake the sense that something terrible would occur.

Needing to ease her anxiety, Signora Anna called her brother.

"*Ciao, Carlo*," Anna greeted him. "How are you?"

"I'm fine," he replied. "The question is how are you and that poor, sweet Nina?"

Anna's heart sped up once more. She glanced at the clock. "Oh Carlo, I wish you were here to take control of this mess she's in. She's so determined to find her husband. I told her last night that he's not worth this stress."

"And what did she say to that?" Carlo interrupted.

"It falls on deaf ears. For whatever reason, she still loves him."

Carlo was silent for a moment. "You know, sometimes people love for the wrong reasons. Nina might love this bastard because she's scared to stop. Once she does, she'll have to accept that he's rejected her and feel the shame that comes with it, living in an old-fashioned town full of gossips. Or maybe she loves him for the sake of her children. It can't be easy for them without a father. Or—the most obvious reason of all—is that she loves him because she must. He's her only chance at financial security. Remember, her parents have helped her the three years he's been gone. What happens when her parents are no longer here?"

"She thinks she needs him to provide for her and her children," Anna said. The thought tightened her chest with sympathy, and she leaned over to look at Gina playing innocently with her dolls. Where was Lilly now? "I should have called you before she left."

"Why? Where is she?"

"You're not going to believe this, but she's on her way to his house. She had an address."

"What?" Carlo's voice grew loud on the other end. Panic and anger laced his voice. "She went to find this pig by herself?"

"No, of course not. I asked my nephew Matteo to accompany her. He knows not to leave her alone, regardless of whether her husband is there or not."

She could hear Carlo's heavy feet pacing the floor. "What time did she leave?"

"About an hour ago, but the driver had to stop for Matteo first. I also instructed the driver to wait for them and bring them straight back here. Nina and the girls are staying with me."

"Okay, don't worry," Carlo said, voice calm again. "You did all the right things. What neighborhood is this address?"

"It's in Coney Island."

"Son of a bitch!" Carlo slammed his hand down on a counter on his end. "It was infested with drugs when I lived in New York. Just like him to live in such a slum."

Hearing her brother's panic, Signora Anna's anxiety returned in force. She felt responsible for Nina and her daughters now. "I shouldn't have sent her. I should've tried harder to stop her—"

"No, no," Carlo assured her, realizing that his response had made her nervous. "Listen, just give me the address. I'll call Nick and tell him to go and wait for them there. He lives in Brooklyn too."

"Yes, of course." Anna found where she'd written the location and gave it to her brother.

Carlo promised to send his godson. He had no idea that his intervention was unnecessary in this instance.

After all, Nick was already heading to the address on Nina's paper. It was his home.

* * *

Nina clutched Lilly's hand as they approached the house.

Anna's nephew Matteo had already been picked up and sat beside them in the Mercedes. Nina was his aunt's good friend, and he'd been nothing but cordial and polite to them both.

The driver looked at the house numbers, comparing them to the address on his paper. "This is it."

The car stopped before an old house whose exterior was a blend of white stucco and green wood siding. Boxes cluttered the long cement steps leading to the porch.

Nina took a deep breath, squeezed her daughter's hand, and climbed from the car. Matteo, obeying his aunt's instructions, followed.

They reached the porch. A button doorbell hung from a thin wire. Nina's eyes locked on it. Her heart pounded in her chest, but she didn't hesitate.

Nina rang the doorbell.

The soft chime came from within. Lilly clutched the edge of her mother's skirt. They waited.

No one came to the door.

Nina pushed the doorbell again, holding her finger down until the chime stretched into a loud, obnoxious screech.

There was a mutter and the sound of footsteps within. Nina released the doorbell, trying to hear more. Had that been her husband?

The door swung open.

A beautiful, dark-haired woman dressed in jeans and a tight-fitted blouse stood before her.

It was Carmen.

Nina's brow furrowed. *Do I have the wrong house or—?*

A lump rose in Nina's throat. She worried her heart might stop. Not knowing English, she turned to Matteo. "Please, ask this woman if Nicola Niceli lives here and who she is to him?"

Matteo, stuck in the middle with little idea about what was occurring, translated Nina's question into English.

"Who the hell is she that I have to answer to her?" Carmen asked, being feisty and waving her hand at Nina without looking at her. Who did this strange woman think she was? Interrupting her morning by asking for her boyfriend?

Matteo knew the answer without needing to translate. "She is Nicola Niceli's wife, and this is his daughter, Lilly."

Carmen glanced down at the little girl at Nina's legs. Lilly's face was buried in her mother's skirts. Carmen didn't recognize her as the same child she'd played with at the *castillo*, but the dark curls did remind her of Nick.

Carmen studied the visitor. His wife's sudden appearance could mean trouble for Nick. If what this woman said was true, she needed to leave, quick. Fortunately he was out.

"Tell her he doesn't live here," she lied.

But it was too late to distract with lies. Over the woman's shoulder, Carmen saw Nick coming down the block.

* * *

Nick strutted like a cool cat as he approached his house. He noticed some commotion on his porch. He squinted and tried to make out what was going on. Carmen appeared to be arguing with a man and a woman, but their backs were to him.

He climbed the steps. Carmen caught his eye and twitched her head in a different direction. *Keep walking.* But Nick didn't catch the hint.

Even with Nina less than four feet away, he hadn't recognized her.

Nick didn't understand Carmen's warning. The first hint he had as to what was occurring was Lilly.

The little girl turned her head as he approached, eyes wide and anxious. Beautiful dark curls twisted around her head.

Nick froze. A memory flashed through his mind of a hot summer day in a pool in Puerto Rico. It couldn't be the same little girl. Why would she be on his porch?

Then Nick noticed something that had escaped him before.

She looks like me.

But it couldn't be. That was impossible. And yet—

Nick's heart raced to the edge of cardiac arrest. He moved forward, stepping onto the porch. His hand grabbed Nina's shoulder and spun her around, the same way he had when he first kissed her in the kitchen of her aunt's home.

This time, there was no kiss.

The sight of Nina's face was a knife slicing through his chest. It was so visceral that, for a second, he felt he'd truly been stabbed.

For Nina, it was as though she'd been hit by a freight train. She hadn't known it was possible to feel so many emotions at once—anger, relief, contempt, love, and perhaps foolishly, a little bit of hope. Experiencing them knocked the wind out of her. She gasped, feeling as though all the oxygen had vanished from the earth. If she didn't get some air in her lungs, she worried she'd pass out.

Why can't I hate him? I want to hate him.

Instead, Nina wanted to wrap him in her arms. She felt the urge to kiss him, not sexually, but in the way a mother might kiss a son returning from war.

"How did you get here?" Nick dropped his hand from her shoulder. His voice was cold and abrupt.

Tears gushed from Nina's eyes. Over three years apart, and that was the first thing he said to her?

With rage and anger, Nina said, "That's really not important right now, is it?"

"But—"

"Do you have any idea what you put me through?" she hissed. She hoped that he couldn't hear her voice trembling.

"I didn't mean to hurt you."

"Hurt me? Are you crazy saying that? You knew very well what you were doing! You were killing me slowly, every single day, for the last three and a half years!"

Signora Anna had warned Nina to prepare for the worst, and yet she couldn't believe what was happening. Wrapped up in the moment, she forgot about the others on the porch, even Lilly, who trembled behind her skirt.

Nina took a deep breath and wiped her face with both hands. More composed, she stepped back and looked her husband. Even though her heart refused to release him, her eyes burned with contempt and disgust.

"*Porco!*" Nina shouted. "*Porco Bastardo!* You dirty, filthy pig! If you needed to see a whore, maybe I could have understood. We could have moved on. But instead, you stop calling and stop writing and even stop sending money. You abandon your own children! How could you do that? What happened to you? Was this your choice?"

Nick's mouth opened and closed like a dying fish. He had neither the strength nor courage to answer her.

"And you!" Nina screamed at the top of her lungs as she spun to face Carmen. "You whore! You had to have known that he has not one, not two, but three little girls. We survived only because of the kindness of my parents. They fed his children the entire time this *porco bastardo* was with you!"

Nick had no explanation for his own actions, but he summoned the courage to speak now that his beloved Carmen was under attack—even if she couldn't understand the insults Nina hurled at her in Sicilian.

"Lower your voice," Nick said, stepping forward to place himself between his wife and his love. "We'll talk tomorrow. Where are you staying? I'll come to you so we can talk."

Nina ignored him, too furious to communicate. Despite being only five feet tall, she seemed to tower above the others on the porch, burning with rage.

Matteo made himself small in a corner, eager to leave. He didn't know what his aunt had gotten him involved in, but he couldn't wait to get home.

The usually fiery Carmen sank against the wall. She couldn't think of a sarcastic or biting comment appropriate for the occasion.

Nina wished the other woman would speak, however. She was ready to chew her up and spit her out. At least, until Lilly caught her attention.

Beneath Nina's skirt, Lilly sobbed, tears streaming down her cheeks.

She'd been silently listening to the exchange and couldn't contain herself any longer.

Nina reached down and lifted her daughter into her arms, pulling her close to her chest.

Nick should've been moved by the sight of his wife caring for their daughter. Instead, his stomach turned with discomfort and guilt.

"It's okay, baby," Nina said, running a hand over Lilly's hair. "I'm sorry."

"Is this my father?" Lilly managed to ask, looking at Nick through her tears.

Nina hesitated, but she couldn't lie. "Yes, he is." She braced for the next painful question her daughter would ask: *Why doesn't he want to be with us? Does he not love us?*

But Lilly said something else. "Why didn't you tell us when he played with us in the pool?" she asked.

Nina's brow furrowed. "What are you talking about, dear?"

"When we stayed with Signore Carlo," Lilly said. She lifted her hand and pointed at both Nick and Carmen. "They took care of Gina and me when you went to the hospital with Signora Anna."

Carmen's eyes widened with recognition. Though she didn't speak Italian, she'd understood the names. She crept forward and whispered something into Nick's ear.

In those moments, the pieces began connecting for Nina.

"Mamma, mamma—" said Lilly, crying now.

Nina didn't hear her. She just stared at her husband. He'd met their daughters at the *castillo*, and his name in America was Nick.

"You son a bitch—you're Signore Carlo's godson!" she yelled.

There was no sense in denying it. Nick had already deduced the connection, though he'd hoped Nina wouldn't. "And you were the young mother staying at the *castillo*—"

"Yes, I am. Signore Carlo was sympathetic to my situation—unlike *you*!" Nina shouted, jabbing a finger at his chest.

"Nina—" he said.

She cut him off. "I think he'd be fascinated to learn that the filthy pig who abandoned his wife and daughters is none other than his beloved godson, don't you?"

"Listen—"

There was nothing to listen to. Her daughter was crying now, clutching Nina's leg. Nina clutched her fists and threw her head back as an animalistic scream exploded from her throat.

Then, perhaps from the stress of having experienced so many emotions in such a short space, Nina stopped screaming. Instead, she started to laugh.

Chapter Nineteen

"Hey, Nina, listen to me." Nick waved his hand before her face. Nina kept laughing. She couldn't help it.

"Let's talk tomorrow," Nick said again. "Where are you staying?"

Nina's laughter stopped. It went into silence. Her mouth twisted into a small, cold smile. She clutched Lilly tight so she couldn't look up and see the contempt in her mother's expression—or realize that it was only a mask for more tears.

"I'm staying with Signora Anna," Nina said coolly. "I'm sure your godfather can give you the address."

With that parting blow, Nina carried Lilly down the steps, followed by a relieved Matteo. In the car, Anna's driver waited patiently.

Once her daughter was safely within, Nina took one last look at her husband, gaping at them from the porch. Their eyes met.

All the feelings crashed into Nina once more.

If he cared or had any decency, he'd be coming with us right now. Nick, what happened to you, you bastard?

Tears streamed from Nina's face. She hid the hurt behind a final shout of anger. "You bastard! You pig bastard!"

With those final words, Nina climbed into the car and slammed the door.

* * *

Nina held her daughter tight as they drove toward Manhattan.

The driver had already dropped off Matteo at his home. It had taken all of Nina's strength not to bawl her eyes out with him in the car. Signora Anna's poor nephew had been a nervous wreck. He'd never been in the middle of such a heated argument.

Now that it was just her and Lilly, tears rolled down Nina's face. She stifled the sobs so that her daughter wouldn't notice.

The driver had informed Signora Anna that they were on their way back, but Nina hadn't shared the details. Nick's words had rattled her initial confidence. As lovely a person as Signore Carlo was, Nina couldn't be certain he would side with her over his own godson. And if that were the case, would sweet Signora Anna still want to put up with them?

If the worst was truly to occur, Nina wanted to know sooner. She asked the driver to use the car phone to call Signore Carlo.

The old man answered on the first ring, surprising Nina. She'd expected Felipe. "Signore Carlo, is that you?"

He recognized her voice. "Nina? Yes, it is me. Are you safe?"

"I found the pig," she said, running her fingers through Lilly's curls to stop her tears. She couldn't tell the old man what happened if she was sobbing. "I had an address. He lives there with his mistress. She must have known he was married with three daughters, but I guess she didn't care."

Nina couldn't see it, but Carlo's hand tightened into a fist on the other end. "I'm so sorry, my sweet child."

"Thank you." Nina took a breath. "But Signore Carlo, I have to tell you the truth. You actually know my husband."

Silence from the other end. Then: "I do?"

"Yes. He's your godson. In America, he goes by the name Nick Niceli."

There was more silence. Nina feared the worst. Certainly he must feel as betrayed by his godson as she did.

"I understand if you don't wish to help me anymore," Nina said, unable to stop her sobs. "And I still thank you for your incredible kindness. Everything you've done for us—"

"Nina, listen to me and respect what I'm about to tell you." Carlo's voice was firm but kind. "Take your little girl and go home to Anna. Stay there. I'll fly up in a couple of days, and I'll take care of this."

With that parting promise, Carlo ended the call.

* * *

The door to the penthouse swung open.

Signora Anna waited in the foyer. She'd already received calls from both her nephew and her brother.

Nina sent Lilly to check on her sister, then rushed straight into the older woman's arms. Her cry was that of a wounded child.

"*Figlia mia,*" Signora Anna said, holding Nina close. "I heard what happened. I'm hurting so much for you. I don't know what to say or do. Let's go to the kitchen. I'll fix you a cup of chamomile tea."

Nina continued sobbing, relieved to no longer need to hold back her tears. "Signora Anna, I had no idea that he was living with another woman. I wouldn't have gone. I swear I wouldn't have."

Signora Anna put Nina to sit on the stool while she fixed the cup of tea.

"He didn't even acknowledge his own daughter, and she was crying. Heartless, ice-cold bastard. Do you know he had the audacity to say he didn't mean to hurt me?"

Anna handed her the tea and said nothing. This was the time to listen.

"Oh Signora Anna, if I live to be one hundred, I'll never calm down. And if I do, I'll just remind myself of what I've been through so I can feel this anger always and forever. Do you know the bastard is your brother's godson? He was at the *castillo* with us. This whole time, I thought it was a kind stranger who babysat my daughters. It was *their own father!*"

Signora Anna shook her head, barely believing it herself. "Carlo wanted to call Nick to help you. It's a good thing he never managed to connect."

"No, then the bastard would've had warning," Nina agreed, finally wrapping her hand around the handle of the teacup. She took a sip. "You should've seen his face when he saw me. I thought he was going to have a heart attack."

"I want to hear all about it later," Signora Anna assured her. "For now, let's worry about the children." She tilted her head toward the doorway.

Lilly and Gina had come downstairs. Both peeped at their mother from the edge of a doorway.

Nina's heart broke at the sight of her daughters. They looked so scared and anxious.

"You're right, Signora Anna," she said. "I've been ignoring their feelings all because of that bastard."

As mothers often must, Nina forced a smile, trying to hide her anger and despair from her children. She went to them and swept them into her arms.

The girls were tired, especially Lilly. She'd spent most of the day in tears, and though she couldn't express it, her emotions were as tumultuous as her mother's own. No child should have to experience what she had.

Nina spent the day playing with her daughters before putting them to bed after an early dinner. She kissed both of them goodnight and thought to herself, *Tomorrow is another day.*

Chapter Twenty

The next day was quieter and more pleasant. Nina chatted and assisted her new friend with different tasks about the penthouse while the children played upstairs. That evening, Signora Anna herself prepared their dinner.

They'd just finished eating when the intercom rang.

Signora Anna's head snapped up, suddenly alert. "Go upstairs to the bedroom," she said. "I don't know who this might be."

Lilly and Gina were upset. They'd been waiting for ice cream sundaes in tall tulip glasses. Instead, Nina cleared the table quickly, then took her daughters upstairs, avoiding the wait for the elevator.

Again, the intercom rang.

Signora Anna picked up the receiver. On the other end was the doorman downstairs.

"Yes, George?"

"I'm sorry to disturb you. I have a gentleman here who wishes to talk to you and Signora Nina. He says his name is Nick Niceli. Shall I allow him to come up?"

"Hold on a few minutes. Let me check with Ms. Nina."

Anna ran to Nina's bedroom, where she knew they would all be. She knocked on the door and called out her name.

"Nina, open. It's me, honey."

Recognizing the voice, Nina opened the door. "Tell me."

"It's him. It's up to you if you want to see him."

From the look Signora Anna gave her, there was no question who she meant.

Nina glanced at her daughters. They'd gathered with their dolls around a tea set to indulge in fake dessert.

"Is he alone?" Nina whispered.

Signora Anna nodded.

"Let him up."

* * *

Nick was already upstairs when Nina came into the kitchen. He sat on one of the stools in the kitchen, tapping his hand against his knee. Signora Anna sat beside him, engaged in polite but cold conversation.

"Nina." Nick stood the moment he saw her. "How are you? Can we talk in private?"

"Why? There's no sense in privacy now. Everyone knows what you did to me." Nina's eyes were cold as she looked at her husband, but the anger from the previous day burned within her. "Besides, I have no secrets from Signora Anna. If you want to talk, the stage is all yours."

Nick's hand closed into a fist about his curls. He didn't understand this woman before him. "When did you become so bold? You used to be such a private person."

"When did I become so bold?" Nina couldn't believe he needed to ask. "You abandoned us and left me to fend for myself and our children in town alone. Do you know the shame that put me through? I had to get used to it. So, if you have anything to say, say it now. I've become immune to shame and being bold is all I know."

Nick stared in disbelief. This was not the Nina he'd left back home.

Signora Anna remained silent. It wasn't her place to interject, but she was proud of how Nina was handling her husband.

I just hope her heart doesn't make her surrender, Signora Anna thought.

Nick ran his hand through his curls. He hadn't expected an audience, and feeling the old woman watching made him nervous. Still, he had to start somewhere.

"Nina, how old were we when we got married?"

"Where are you going with this?"

Nick wanted to explain how he'd felt about the situation, then and now. However, the sound of little footsteps interrupted him.

Lilly and Gina had followed their mother downstairs. The two little girls peeped into the kitchen.

All the words he'd intended to say caught in Nick's throat.

My daughters.

Nick's heart pounded with unexpected force. He felt a sudden desire to embrace them. But they must hate him now. He recalled playing with them in the pool—Lilly riding on his shoulders, Gina giggling as he lost his shoe.

How could I not recognize my own children?

Disgust turned Nick's stomach. He'd never hated himself more.

Nina crossed her arms. Her stare was colder than the iceberg that hit the Titanic. "You were saying?"

"What I want to say doesn't involve the kids," Nick managed.

"Really? The girls shouldn't know where their father's been these past three years? Or did you want to tell them you were out delivering Christmas gifts with Santa Claus?"

"I see you've become sarcastic as well."

"Thanks to you, Nicola."

The phone rang, interrupting their conversation, which was a relief to Nick. This wasn't going how he'd planned.

Signora Anna stepped away to take the call on the balcony.

Lilly and Gina crept forward to stand beside their mother. They stared from behind her legs, their expressions a mixture of curiosity and confusion.

Words escaped Nick again.

Nina rested a protective hand on each of her daughters. Her eyes remained on her husband. Emotions raged within her at the sight of him still. Now that they were all in the kitchen, almost a family again, she couldn't find words either.

The kitchen remained silent, save for the muffled whispers of

Signora Anna's voice on the balcony followed by soft footsteps when she returned.

"That was Carlo. He's flying in tomorrow," she informed them. "I mentioned you were here, Nick. He wants to see you tomorrow night."

Nick's eyes widened. He'd rather eat fire than face his godfather now.

His reluctance was evident. Signora Anna held up her hands. "I did my part by delivering the message. It's up to you if you come or not."

Nick's stomach turned. He'd wanted to get things sorted with his wife quickly and privately.

Nina had no such objections. She gave Nick a cold smile. "Then we'll talk tomorrow."

Nick sighed. There was no sense trying to discuss the matter with Nina now. He ought to leave, but his eyes kept flicking towards his daughters.

"Do you remember me?" Nick crouched down and called them with a wave of his fingers. "We played together. In Puerto Rico."

Nina didn't try to stop the girls as they tiptoed toward him. After all, they should know their father.

Nick reached for their hands. Gina snapped hers away and ran back to her mother. Lilly, meanwhile, accepted the gesture with a shy smile. The resemblance between her and her father was unmistakable.

"You know, you've got my hair," Nick said, feeling more comfortable and resting his palm on her curls.

Lilly's smile grew a little bigger. "You're my Papa, right?"

Although she couldn't remember her father, she'd always had a soft spot for him. Nick had cared for Lilly when Nina was pregnant with all her complications. The bond they'd formed remained etched in the little girl's subconscious.

Nina watched the exchange from the corner of her eye. She was afraid to stare outright lest Nick notice her feelings. Her mind kept drifting back to Bagheria—when she'd first seen him at her aunt's home, their secret meetings in the abandoned barn. Who could have known how much life would change?

"She looks just like me, doesn't she?" Nick said, addressing Signora Anna. "And the little one is the image of Nina."

Caught off guard by his cordiality, Signora Anna responded in kind. "Yes. Gina is a spitfire too, just like her mother."

Gina beamed with pride at the comparison.

Nick laughed, continuing to speak about his daughters with such warmth and pride it seemed impossible to believe that he'd abandoned them for years.

Listening to him, Signora Anna recalled a piece of wisdom she'd once heard and had shared with Nina on the beach in Caracas. In life, people have different roles they play. A man is a husband, a son, a friend, and so on. In each of his roles, he is different. He may be a bad husband but a loyal friend. Or he may be a cruel son but a caring husband.

Those words seemed truer to Anna than ever before. The older woman also recalled the positive way her brother had spoken of Nick when they were in Puerto Rico.

The time grew later. Nick stood and made excuses to leave.

Lilly clung to his hand. "Papa, when will I see you again? Why can't you sleep here? You can have my bed, and I'll share with Gina."

Nick's heart broke at the request. "I can't. I forgot to bring my pajamas. And Gina is tough. She may not want anyone in her bed. She scares me."

Lilly laughed. "She doesn't scare me."

"I have to go to work in the morning, but I'll be back here tomorrow night. I promise." Nick drew a finger across his heart.

He and Nina exchanged polite goodnights. Then Nick turned to Anna.

"Goodnight, Signora. Thank you for allowing me to come up. I will try to be here when my godfather arrives tomorrow night. I am sorry for any inconvenience I may have caused you. *Buona note e grazie.*"

With that parting farewell, Nick stepped outside and onto the elevator.

When the doors closed behind him, Nina burst into tears.

Chapter Twenty-One

Signora Anna prepared everything for her brother's arrival. A hairstylist came to the penthouse and worked on both Nina and Anna's hair. Even the kids got their bangs trimmed.

The night's dinner was prepared by Donatello, one of the best Sicilian chefs in the city. He happened to be free that night and accepted the job out of respect for Signore Carlo. When Donatello first arrived in New York, it was Carlo who'd gotten him a job as assistant head chef.

Signora Anna and Nina weren't the only ones excited about Signore Carlo's impending arrival. Upon hearing the news, George the doorman burst into a massive smile. "*Oh dios mio, qué sorpresa!* I haven't felt this happy in a long time!"

Upon Carlo's return, the reason for George's joy became clear.

"Still working in this same building, ah?" Carlo asked, greeting the doorman as he stepped into the building.

"But of course, Signore Stefano!"

Carlo smiled, took five hundred-dollar bills from his pocket, and gave them to George. "Take your wife out to dinner one night. Enjoy each other now, while you're both healthy."

George's thanks were profusive. Almost crying, he wrapped Carlo in a hug. The old man was relieved no one was around to see.

Carlo took the elevator straight up to the penthouse, where the others waited in the foyer to greet him.

* * *

When the elevator doors opened, Nina held back, letting Signora Anna be the first to embrace her brother. Only after the two had properly said hello did she go to Carlo. She hugged him and kissed his face like only a daughter does. Then, Lilly and Gina rushed to the old man.

Love is earned and then given back. Signore Carlo earned the love from those kids by giving them happiness in Puerto Rico, and in return, the kids loved him back.

The old man carried a grinning Lilly and Gina to sit with him on the couch, and Nina's heart swelled with pride. To have Signore Carlo and Signora Anna in their lives was a privilege and an honor. Nina didn't feel worthy of them.

And where is my husband? He's made such a mess of our lives.

Soon, dinner was to be served. Despite his previous offer to arrive before his godfather, there was no sign of Nick.

Delicious as the meal was, and happy as she was to see Carlo, Nina's thoughts drifted to her husband throughout the meal.

I never should've let him touch me.

Everything began with that damn kiss in the kitchen. Why was she so desperate to have a boyfriend at such a young age? Where were the adults throughout his whole thing? She used to sneak out and meet him. Had her parents never noticed, or did they close their eyes because Nick came from money?

"Donatello is a genius in the kitchen, don't you think, Nina?" Carlo asked.

The question pulled Nina from her thoughts. She forced a smile, not wanting to offend the kind siblings who'd welcomed her by being unpleasant. "Dinner is incredible," she agreed.

Carlo smiled, then spoke to his sister.

Nina tried to wrangle her drifting thoughts and focus on the conversation with little success. She was rescued by the sudden buzz of the intercom.

Nick had kept his word.

* * *

Nina's heart rate spiked from eighty to eight hundred as the door opened.

Nick entered the penthouse looking sharp and well-dressed. He greeted Carlo with a huge smile.

But this was not the same godfather he'd visited in Puerto Rico.

"Nicholas, you came." Carlo nodded his head, acknowledging his godson without warmth.

Nick's face was like a puppy who'd been kicked. He deserved it. Yet the sight stung Nina's heart.

Nick embraced his godfather and took a seat. "How was your trip?"

"I had hoped my return to New York would be for more pleasurable reasons," Carlo said, dabbing the corners of his mouth with his napkin. "But under the circumstances, the plane ride was fine, thank you."

Nick shifted in his seat, like a criminal about to be sentenced.

Nina almost wanted to be his defense attorney. She had to stop and remind herself, *I'm the one who's put him on trial.*

The usual warmth and love on Carlo's face had been replaced by steel. There were no displays of emotions as he spoke with his godson. An aura of authority and discipline radiated from the older man.

None of this reflected the truth of Carlo's heart. He longed to embrace Nick. Even though he was devastated, he still loved him like a son.

But weakness was not meant for men. Carlo could not let his resolve be softened by his love for his godson.

"Niceli and I need to have a private conversation," Carlo said. "Where can we go, Anna?"

* * *

Signora Anna had a private office in the bottom floor of the penthouse. Walls and a solid door separated it from the rest of the rooms.

Carlo sat in the burgundy leather seat behind the desk. Nick took a smaller chair, sitting before him like a child sent to the principal's office.

The old man rested his elbows on the desk. His hands clutched one another in a tight fist. "Can you tell me what the fuck you've done?"

Nick flinched. He hadn't expected his godfather to speak to him in this manner, and Carlo's anger only grew.

"You abandoned your wife and your three daughters? Three little girls? Have you gone completely mad and lost your mind? What the fuck happened to you?"

Carlo's voice was rising.

"Godfather, please—"

"Don't you dare call me that!" Carlo shouted. "Right now, you are my worst enemy. You had the audacity to come into my house and make a fool out of me. How dare you come to my home with your mistress? You know what we call her in Sicily! A *puttana*! You made me think she was your longtime girlfriend. You never mentioned your wife and children! Did the Puerto Rican sun melt your brain?"

"I—"

"Oh, you didn't forget, you son of a bitch! You knew I would never condone your behavior, especially in my own home!"

Nick's tan had fled, leaving him as pale as a ghost.

"If I didn't know your parents were decent people, I'd think you were the son of a whore, *figlio di buttana*. Niceli, listen to me. You know me well. You've seen my estate. I have the power to cripple you for life. So, listen to what I say and listen good, because I will only say it once. *Hai capito?*"

A lump rose in Nick's throat. He nodded.

"You will go out there and tell your wife that you're going to find a house to rent or buy for you and your family. You will live there as husband and wife. You will provide for them. Put the kids in school and continue with your work. Live a happy life with your family. What you do in your spare time with your mistress is your business. But if you disrespect or hurt Nina, then it will become my business. *U capisti?*"

"I understand."

"Do you? Because I swear, Niceli, I will cripple you, your mistress, and anyone who comes after."

A cold chill washed over Nick. He felt hollow and lifeless. If he stood, he'd hit the floor. Hard.

"Please, hear me out," he pleaded, voice barely above a whisper.

"You have sixty seconds."

Nick took a deep breath. He tried to remember what he'd wanted to say to Nina when he'd come to see her the previous day. "We were both very young when we got married. You know how it is in Sicily. We eloped because she got pregnant, and I had no choice—"

"You're saying you were forced into the marriage."

"Yes." Nick felt a moment of relief. "That's exactly right."

"And were you also forced to pull your pants down and get her pregnant?"

"I—" Nick faltered for a response.

"Don't tell me she forced you or I will punch that shit excuse out of your mouth for trying to make a fool out of me again. You fathered three daughters. Not one. Three." He held up his fingers as though he doubted Nick's ability to count. "Get the fuck out of here."

Nick scrambled to his feet.

"And Niceli?" Carlo's voice had gone even colder than before.

The sound chilled Nick to the bone, freezing him to the spot.

"After tonight, don't show your face to me again," Carlo said. "Not if you value your life."

Chapter Twenty-Two

When they left Anna's private office, they found two new guests in the living room. Both were men, dressed in sharp suits. They lounged on the furniture as though they'd visited the penthouse before.

Nick's heart nearly stopped. He recognized one of them as an underboss from one of the most powerful crime families in New York.

What the fuck is he doing here?

Carlo greeted both men with a big smile. The underboss kissed his hand.

Then, Nick understood. His godfather had invited these men to prove a point. If a crime boss was kissing his hand, Carlo hadn't been exaggerating his power.

A shiver went through Nick. For the first time in his life, he knew what it was to be truly afraid.

* * *

Nick remained silent throughout the meal, a ghost sipping espresso and Sambuca at the end of the table. He explained that he'd had

Nick tapped Nina's elbow, leaned close, and whispered. "Let's go somewhere we can talk."

Nina might have refused, but she didn't wish to cause a scene in front of Carlo's guests. Even being from another country, she could tell they weren't altar boys.

Had Carlo summoned them on her behalf? Did they know about the situation with Nick?

The thought terrified Nina. She didn't want her husband hurt.

Nina nodded and stood.

Nick followed suit, inclining his head politely to the men at the table. "Will you excuse us? My wife and I need to talk."

Perhaps they were altar boys after all. At the same time, both men bowed their heads, and chorused, "By all means."

Nina led Nick to the balcony, now her favorite place in the penthouse.

He ran his hand through his curls, barely stopping himself from pacing.

"I know I put you through hell, Nina, but that wasn't my intention. I can't ask you to forgive me, but I'm begging you, at least help me so we can live in peace."

Nina raised her eyebrows. After everything, he had the gall to ask for her help?

"Remember when I started to say how young we were when we eloped? You got annoyed and became sarcastic. But all I was trying to say was that we made a lot of mistakes. We were doing things at such a young age."

"You were the one begging me for it."

"Please, let me finish." He raised his hands. "We should have stayed together for a while, gotten engaged, seen if we really loved each other."

"You seem to have forgotten a lot since leaving Bagheria. Let me remind you. Diana's not here, but you have another child. Would we have told our unborn child to stay put? Papa's not ready to get married?"

"No—"

"Or did you want her to be born out of wedlock to shame me? Is that it? Go on, hit me with your next excuse."

Nick tapped his foot. This was not the wife he'd left in Sicily. She'd become smart, mature, and sarcastic.

"No more? Good. Then let's get to the bottom line. What you're trying to tell me is that you never loved me. You're saying that you'd rather be with that dirty piece of shit? Fine. But I'm not going away. I'm not going back to Bagheria to be shamed all over again."

Nick's voice was soft. "I never said I never loved you."

The anger retreated from Nina's face. Her heart pounded. She became a young girl, staring at him with doe eyes once more. She hoped he'd say more, profess that he still harbored some kind feelings for her.

Perhaps he had desired her for a while, back in Sicily, but those feelings had disappeared. Whatever his feelings were now, they were irrelevant. He had no choice but to follow his godfather's orders.

"Tomorrow, we'll go house hunting," he told her. "Or rent an apartment. We'll live together as a family. I'll work and provide for you and the girls, but you have to understand that I have tons of jobs in other states. I'll show you the contracts, but I can't be home every night. Can you accept that?"

"What about the *puttana*?"

"Why must you be so nasty?" Nick had hoped she wouldn't ask about Carmen. "She helped me get on my feet and found jobs for me in the beginning."

"So why is she still around if you have tons of jobs?"

"Because now we're friends."

Nina didn't want to cry, so she laughed at this pathetic excuse. "Oh well, excuse me. If she's your friend, she's my friend too. Maybe I should thank her for being such a good *friend* to my husband. What do you say? Should I invite her over and make a hot cup of poison?"

Nick couldn't continue to discuss Carmen lest he let his real emotions get the better of him. He loved her, and it pained him what his godfather was forcing him to do.

"What are you doing tonight?" he asked Nina. "Are we sleeping here, or do you want to go to a hotel with the kids?"

The sudden shift shocked Nina. "I didn't think you wanted to spend the night with us."

"If you want to stay here, I have no problem with that. She must have a room for me too. Just go get my kids and help me make peace with the little one. I'm still her father."

"I see that your memory is coming back, eh Nicola?"

Nick smiled. It didn't feel as forced when he was talking about his children. "The little one is a carbon copy of you. Lilly is in my corner."

"For now," Nina said, but her tone made it clear she was teasing. She returned Nick's smile, scarcely able to believe what was happening.

We're going to be a family again.

* * *

Nina's face was red from excitement when she ran into the living room.

Anna and Carlo sat alone on the couches, reminiscing about their youth in Sicily. The other two men had left.

"You'll never believe it," Nina said, crouching to speak with Signora Anna. "He's a different man. He must have fallen, hit his head, and realized what he'd done. He wants to come back into our lives. He wants us to live together as a family. Can you believe it?"

Signore Carlo was the happiest of the three. He had no desire to punish his wayward godson. He nodded his approval at Nick as he returned inside.

Nina took her husband's wrist. "Come, let's tell the girls."

The two children had been sent upstairs before Carlo's other guests arrived. They'd already changed into their pajamas and were playing on the bed.

Lilly was overjoyed to see her papa upstairs, and even more excited to learn he would be sleeping in the house with them.

"Papa, why can't you sleep in here with us?" she asked.

Nick smiled. "Because we won't all fit in one bed. Besides, I snore. Would you like to hear me all night long?"

Lilly giggled and shook her head. "No, Papa, you're right. You sleep in the other room."

It never crossed her mind that her father wanted to be apart from them because he was anxious to call his mistress.

* * *

Nick waited until he was certain his wife and daughters were fast asleep before tiptoeing down the stairs.

Even with Carlo's threats hanging over him, Nick was certain of one thing: He loved Carmen.

I can't live without her.

Nick crept into the kitchen, found the phone in the dark, and dialed Carmen's number.

There was no answer. Carmen must have fallen asleep waiting for him to come home.

What is she going to think?

Nick decided to try her once more.

His mind spun with concern as he dialed the number a second time. Nick didn't notice the soft footsteps entering the kitchen behind him.

Signora Anna had come downstairs to get a glass of water. However, she stopped when she saw Nick. His back was to her, and the phone pressed against his ear. The old woman pressed her back to the wall, debating whether to go in or return to her room.

Carmen answered this time, her voice thick with sleep.

"My love, there you are." Nick sighed in relief at the sound of her. "I'm so sorry. I can't talk for long. This is the first chance I've had to call you. I saw Carlo this evening."

"Aw, your godfather is there? Give him my love."

"I don't think so," Nick said. "The old man is more powerful than God, trust me. And he took a liking to Nina when she stayed with him. He's forcing me—"

Nick's voice caught. How could he tell her that his godfather had threatened to hurt her if he didn't reunite with his wife?

"I'll explain when I see you in person," Nick said. "I'll come as soon as I can, I promise. Please, be patient until then. I love you, Carmen, more than life. I always will."

He pressed the receiver and ended the call.

Signora Anna hid behind the wall unit in the living room, holding her breath as she watched Nick return upstairs. Her heart broke for Nina. The poor girl had such high hopes. Hearing what her husband had just said to his mistress would crush her.

I can't do that to her, Signora Anna thought. *I can't tell her.*

Nothing good would come of it if she did. Her brother didn't make idle threats. Nick might end up dead.

Chapter Twenty-Three

Lilly and Gina woke before their father.
Outside it was a beautiful spring day, and their mother got them cleaned and dressed. Then the two rushed from the room.

Curls loose around her face, Lilly skipped toward her father's room. Gina followed, no idea where they were going. She was just happy to be with her sister.

Lilly knocked on the door.

Gina's brow furrowed. "Why are you knocking? Nobody's in there."

Lilly kept smiling. Perhaps her younger sister hadn't been paying attention to what happened the night before.

"Come in," Nick's voice called from within.

Gina's eyes grew wide and startled. Lilly pushed open the door and bounded toward him.

Nick sat on the edge of the bed. At the sight of his daughters, he beamed and spread his arms, catching Lilly in a hug.

Gina remained, wide-eyed and panicked in the doorway.

At the sight of her, Lilly started giggling. Nick found it impossible not to join her.

This response angered Gina even more. She placed her hands on her hips, glaring at them with an impressive pout. "Why are you laughing, you silly idiots? I hate you, Lilly. And you too, curly-haired man!"

Nick covered his mouth with his hand, trying to muffle his laughter. "Maybe we shouldn't laugh anymore, Lilly. She'll beat us up."

Lilly's giggles grew louder.

A frustrated Gina stomped her foot and marched off, only to return a minute later with her mother.

Nina held her youngest daughter's hand, letting herself be pulled toward the room. Within, Lilly remained seated on her father's knee.

The sight made Nina's heart beat with a joy that she'd almost abandoned hope of feeling again.

"She'll come if you ignore her," she said to Nick, flicking her eyes down to Gina. "But if you give her attention, she'll fight you."

Nick was dying to snatch up his youngest daughter and kiss her endlessly. Her rebellion against him was driving him mad. But he took his wife's advice and ignored her for the time being, riding the elevator down with only Lilly.

At least his middle daughter was eager to spend time with him. Lilly explained all the details of the house to him as they descended.

The housekeeper had already prepared breakfast. Waiting plates lined the kitchen island.

Signora Anna was already seated when Nick and Lilly arrived. Nina and Gina took their seats a few moments later. The two had come into the kitchen via the stairs.

"Where is Signore Carlo?" Nick asked as he accepted a cup of espresso from the housekeeper. He kept his voice calm though his eyes darted toward the kitchen entrance, afraid his godfather would appear at any moment.

"He took an early flight back to Puerto Rico this morning," Signora Anna said. "He told me to extend his apologies for not saying goodbye."

Nick could've collapsed in relief. "I'm so sorry to have missed him."

Signora Anna's look made it clear she didn't believe him. The old woman took a bite of a croissant before changing the topic. "I have a friend who's a real estate broker. She's willing to show you all a couple homes to rent or buy even though it's Sunday. Let me know, and I'll call and confirm it with her."

It sounded like a great idea to Nina, but she looked to Nick for approval.

He shrugged. "Yeah, sure, why not? Can we meet her at eleven?"

"Excellent," Signora Anna said, but the situation felt the opposite. The conversation she'd overheard between Nick and Carmen the previous night played on her mind. She didn't trust the man before her and was eager to have him out of her house.

She wished Carlo had offered one of his other homes instead. At least then she'd know Nina would be safe, and she could kick this no-good bastard out when the time came.

However, when Anna had broached this idea with her brother, he'd refused. Under different circumstances, Carlo would have wanted nothing more than to provide for his godson. However, the old man felt betrayed. He wanted to teach Nick a lesson and force him to step up and provide for his family.

But Carlo had said that Nina could call him whenever she wanted, so long as her husband wasn't nearby. Anna was waiting for a chance to deliver her brother's message to her friend. In the meantime, she forced herself to be polite and cordial with Nick. His charming demeanor made it easier than the old woman wished.

The girls enjoyed chocolate chip pancakes with hot chocolate and whipped cream for breakfast. Nick took Lilly's cup and stole a sip.

"Papa!" the little girl shouted, but it was in delight. She held back a giggle.

Whipped cream coated the tip of Nick's nose and gave him white mustache.

"Something on my face?" he asked.

Even Gina burst into laughter.

Seeing the four of them, sitting around her kitchen island, Signora Anna could almost imagine them to be the happy family Nina wished.

But for all Carlo's power, he couldn't force anyone to fall back in love.

* * *

The real estate agent, Rosa, was the daughter of Signora Anna's close friends. They'd lived in a town near Palermo before immigrating to the United States.

At Signora Anna's recommendation, Rosa took the family of four to search for a new home in Dyker Heights. It was an upper-middle-class neighborhood in Brooklyn, which had historically been occupied by Italian immigrants. The stores and merchants reflected this.

One of the places available for rent was a detached house with lots of land, perfect for the children to play on. It had three bedrooms, a new kitchen, a living room that connected to a formal dining room, one full bathroom, and a half bathroom inside the larger bedroom.

Nina was taken aback, especially when she saw the added laundry room with a washer and dryer.

"Do you like it?" Rosa asked, standing in the center of the living room.

"What's not to like?" Nina replied. She stared through the front window at the tree-lined street beyond. Bells chimed in the distance, signifying the presence of a nearby Roman Catholic church.

"How much is the deposit?" Nick asked. He didn't sound as certain.

"For a friend of Signora Anna's, one month rent will secure the house," Rosa said. "Normally, we require three months and a security deposit, but Signora Anna's vouched for you. Her words are better than John Hancock's signature."

"Oh. Thank you," Nick said politely. "How could anyone refuse an offer like that?"

Despite his words, however, Nick didn't sound excited.

***

The driver took them to the store to purchase furniture next. As they sat in the car, Nick remained silent. He'd signed the paperwork and written the check, but the entire time, his thoughts were on Carmen. Nick needed to see her. He should've been with her, not his wife.

I can't let Carlo get away with this.

Nick had to come up with something, but what?

"Why are you so quiet?" Nina asked. "You haven't said a word since we left Brooklyn."

"I have to pay for this house, for you and the kids," Nick said. "I'm thinking about where and how I can make more money."

Although this hadn't been the focus of Nick's thoughts, there was truth to his lie. As such, Nina believed him easily. The poor thing had no idea Nick had agreed to be a husband again only out of fear.

* * *

They returned to Signora Anna in time for dinner. Sunday dinner was always held at three o'clock in the afternoon, a tradition the old woman refused to skip even though she was outside of Sicily.

The table was already set in the dining room. The cook had prepared *pasta al forno* and meatballs—a favorite of the kids. For seconds, thick pieces of filet mignon and links of freshly made sausage with fennel had been barbequed outside on the terrace.

George had welcomed the family back and called ahead to inform Signora Anna of their return before sending them upstairs. As such, the old woman was waiting in front of the elevator when the doors opened.

Lilly and Gina rushed to her, and Signora Anna wrapped them in her arms.

"And where did you go, Cusciuta?" she asked.

"I'm not Cusciuta. I'm Gina."

"It's a joke," Lilly told her sister. "She's calling you outdoorsy."

Nina told Signora Anna all about the house as they went into the penthouse and sat for dinner.

"You can even hear church bells from inside the house," Nina said, so excited that she'd spent more of dinner talking than eating. "It gave me such a nostalgic feeling of home."

"I'm happy you found something," Anna said. "What about furniture?"

"They'll deliver the beds and couch tomorrow. Everything else will come in the next week."

Signora Anna smiled. She delighted in seeing Nina so excited. Yet every time the older woman looked at Nick, a bitter taste set in her mouth.

Why is he so quiet? Signora Anna wondered.

Nick barely spoke throughout the meal, and when the chance arose, he made an excuse and stepped out on the balcony. Carmen was still on his mind. He couldn't risk calling her while everyone was awake.

He paced the terrace, resentment settling into his heart. With Carlo gone, Nick blamed Nina for his situation.

Why must she pursue a love that's not there? What the hell is wrong with her?

As far as Nick could see, he was the victim in this situation, the one forced to suffer unfairly.

Back inside, Signora Anna leaned close to Nina, whispering so that the girls wouldn't overhear.

"What's Nick's problem? He's acting strange."

"It's only because he has so much on his mind with us here," Nina said, defending him. "He has to pay for all our living expenses, and he's worried about finding more money."

"I guess so," Signora Anna said, but her heart ached. Nick didn't deserve his wife's compassionate defense.

* * *

On Monday morning, Nick woke early. He hurried to get dressed and leave, telling Nina that he had a job in New Jersey.

"I might have an offer to build a mall there," Nick said. "Owners liked my proposal, but we couldn't agree on the labor and construction cost. I'll try make them see reason, but bottom line, I need this job."

Everything Nick was saying was true. He failed to mention, however, that his meeting in New Jersey was at four that afternoon.

The morning, Nick wanted to see Carmen. She didn't work on Mondays.

"Get the kids ready. I'll drop you all off at the new apartment and come back later." It was a nondescript time.

Would later be in another three years? Nina wondered, but she kept her sarcastic response to herself. She was relieved to have her husband back. She wouldn't risk undermining and upsetting him.

At Nick's instructions, Nina hurried and got the girls ready. When they walked out of the building, the girls carried waffles in their hands, eating as they went to the car. Nina hadn't even had time for an espresso.

* * *

When Nina opened the door to her new home, she found a fantastic surprise. Rosa had sent a cleaning crew the previous afternoon, and now the entire house was spotless. Beyond that, there were things already in the fridge: children's snacks, sandwiches, juices, and bottled water.

The realtor had gone above and beyond. She even stopped by around noon to check on Nina and inquire if she needed anything else.

"*Grazie mille, grazie sei molto gentile,*" Nina repeated her thanks to the realtor. She couldn't imagine this was a part of her job.

"Anything for a friend of Signora Anna," Rosa assured her.

* * *

Nick sped toward Coney Island, toward Carmen.

His heart raced with excitement and relief. Finally, he'd broken away from his wife.

Nick skidded into a parking spot, jumped from the car, and ran up the steps. Savoring the thrill of anticipation, he peeped in the kitchen window instead of bursting through the door.

Carmen sat alone, dressed in low, tight-fitted shirt. Her hair fell in waves around her shoulders, and she tapped a painted nail against her cup of coffee.

Nick admired her, his blood rushing further south. He couldn't wait to have her in his arms.

He rang the doorbell, then hid.

Carmen stepped outside and saw no one.

"Fuckers," she whispered. "Probably those kids. Wait till I catch them."

Nick jumped out from behind the door. "How about you catch me instead?"

Carmen screamed—first in shock, then with joy. She flung her arms around his neck and kissed him passionately.

He pushed her back, grinning. "Whoa, if I knew I was coming home to this, I'd have left last night. Get inside before we attract an audience out here."

Nick scooped her into his arms, wrapping one hand around her waist and pulling her close. He couldn't get enough of her.

The feeling was mutual. Their hands pulled at one another's clothing, and their bodies melted together. Nick and Carmen's love had gone beyond physical attraction or simple desire. They burned for one another with intense devotion.

After their passionate lovemaking, Nick sat at the kitchen table while Carmen prepared breakfast.

"I'm in such deep shit," he said, running a hand through his curls. "That prick Carlo flew into New York just to rip my ass. If I had any idea how powerful he is, I'd have stayed away. He's ordered me to be a husband."

Carmen remained by the stove, frying eggs for them, while Nick told her the full story. As she listened, her face grew more concerned. It hadn't occurred to her that the kindly old man from Puerto Rico would threaten her life or have connections with crime bosses.

"He said what I do in my own time is my business," Nick said. "Obviously, he knows I won't give you up. But I don't want to split my time between you and her."

Carmen placed the eggs on the plate and carried them to the table. Her mind spun. They needed a plan.

"Listen," she said, resting the food before Nick. "We can't do anything now but play along with your godfather's game."

Nick couldn't believe what he was hearing. "You want me spending half the time with my wife?"

"Of course not." Keeping her composure, Carmen poured them both cups of coffee. "But if you do what he wants, you can regain Carlo's trust. Tell him what he wants to hear. You were young and made mistakes. Then, when the old man is back in your pocket, we'll find a way to deal with that fucking bitch."

Nick sipped his coffee, trying to follow what Carmen was suggesting.

"Revenge will taste sweeter if you wait for it. You understand, Nick?"

We can savor the anticipation, he thought. That was what he'd just done with her, wasn't it? And it had been all the sweeter for it.

But the thought of living with his wife, pretending to be a loving and devoted husband, staying away from Carmen for stretches of time made Nick's stomach turn.

"I don't want to wait," he said.

"You don't have a choice. We'll still be together, just with little spaces in between. Your job allows you the perfect excuse. Tell her from now on, you'll be coming home only once a week. Maybe even every two weeks."

"I already did."

"Good, tell her the shopping center has a deadline that you must meet. Later, maybe you'll have jobs here in Brooklyn, but she'll think you're in Jersey, Pennsylvania, or Virginia. Your work is your alibi."

"You're so damn good for me. It's no wonder I'm crazy about you," Nick responded like a lovesick puppy.

And so, for the time being, the matter was decided.

* * *

Nina spent her day unpacking. She'd brought a few necessities with her from Sicily: kitchen utensils, clothing, two blankets. She arranged the dishes in the kitchen credenza, taking special care with the cups and the espresso coffee pot.

That afternoon, the beds and couch were delivered. Lilly and Gina wanted to jump on everything. Nina had to stop them before their feet imprinted on the new cushions.

She prepared a simple dinner. There wasn't enough in the kitchen for anything extravagant.

Nina and the girls ate in the kitchen. She got them cleaned and ready for bed.

They were sound asleep by the time their father returned home.

"Took hours for the owners to budge," Nick said as he stomped through the door. It was almost eleven. "But in the end, I profited more than they did."

Nina commended him on his success. She was too excited to be upset about his late arrival, and he'd warned her to expect this.

"Come look at the new furniture," she said.

Nick gave his approval of the couch, and the beds in the girls' rooms as they peeped inside. Then, they came to the last door.

"This is our bedroom," Nina said.

The cruelty in Nick's eyes could have killed. "We never agreed on sleeping together. I'm not that person anymore. I like my freedom, even in bed."

Nina didn't understand. What sort of husband didn't want to sleep with his wife?

"I don't want to discuss it," Nick held up his hand, stopping her before she could argue. "I'm tired, and I need to sleep."

Nina watched as he grabbed a pillow from the bed and carried it toward the couch. Her heart felt as though it had been sliced open.

She hurried to her room so Nick wouldn't see the tears, now gushing down her face.

Nina turned on the sink, letting the water muffle her sobs.

Chapter Twenty-Four

As the days passed, Nina grew more accustomed to American life. She shopped at the nearby supermarket, went to church on Sundays, and became familiar with the local shops on the Avenue. Her daughters too began to think of the house in New York as their home.

One warm morning in May, little Gina wanted a broom to sweep outside.

"That broom is bigger than you," Nina teased her daughter. "You're not going to be able to hold it."

"Will so," Gina insisted.

Amused, Nina fetched the broom from the cupboard and passed it to the feisty little girl.

Gina, struggling just as her mother had predicted, but too determined to let that stop her, swept the patio.

Her efforts caught the attention of Nina's neighbors—a couple who lived across the street.

"That little girl sweeping has to be an Italian little girl," the man said.

His wife, Teresa, came at once to look. She was Italian herself, born in Sicily though she'd moved to the United States when she was seven. Her mother was American-born too, which had made the immigration process smoother and faster for her family. Despite living up in New York, Teresa's family had continued to speak, eat, and do everything in an Italian way. She took great pride in her culture, especially when it came to Sicilian cooking.

Teresa saw little Gina sweeping and determined to meet the parents of the precocious, Italian child.

It was because of this that a strong friendship developed between Teresa and Nina.

* * *

As the bond between them grew, Nina confided in Teresa. She spoke of Sicily, and her life there. She told her the truth of how she'd gotten into the United States.

However, Nina continued to lie about her husband—not about his past abandonment, but his present treatment.

"His behavior is much better now," Nina would say. "Especially toward the children."

Teresa didn't pry, but she had a gut feeling about Nick. He didn't look like a warm, caring father. He showed affection to his daughters, or at least to Lilly, but there was something about him that felt off. Why did he only come home once every two weeks?

"My husband had a big job in New Jersey," Nina said. "He can't come up every day, so the poor guy sacrifices and comes up once a week or every two weeks."

Even if she didn't believe it, Teresa never disagreed with what Nina told her. It wasn't her place.

Instead, Nina's new friend listened. She became a shoulder for Nina to cry on when she missed her oldest daughter or the rest of the family she'd left behind in Bagheria.

To ease the pain, Teresa took Nina to her mother's house.

The old woman had the demeanor of an angel, her closeness to God radiating a warm glow about her person. She offered motherly advice, and showered Nina with affection and warmth. Soon, she became like a second mother to the poor girl, who missed her own family back home.

This connection eased Nina's homesickness and made her trust her neighbor more.

One day while they were sitting in her living room, Nina decided to confide more in Teresa.

"Do you know anyone who might need construction work around here?" Nina inquired. "The reason I ask is that if my husband had a job around here, his kids would be able to see him every day and he could eat with us at the table."

Hearing this question broke Teresa's heart. It didn't take a scientist to figure out that Nina needed her husband too.

That night, Teresa went home and explained everything to her husband, Giacomo. It so happened that he was looking for a good contractor to redo the sidewalk cement around their house and add ceramic tiles in the basement.

When Giacomo approached him about the job, Nick offered such a reasonable price that his neighbor was in disbelief. However, what appeared to be kindness was a calculated ploy. Nick knew of his wife's friendship with Teresa. He didn't want to jeopardize the relationship. After all, the more the neighbors tended to Nina and the children, the easier it was for him to stay away.

* * *

One day, Nick started work on Teresa's sidewalk. Nina watched him from the window, delighted to have him across the street. He even came home for lunch. For Nina, it was like a dream.

Teresa, who'd always been close to her parents, had informed them about the construction work taking place. She'd also mentioned that Giacomo had hired Nina's husband. She didn't use his name.

Otherwise, her parents might have realized that they'd met Nicholas Niceli before.

* * *

Teresa's parents lived only a few blocks away.

On the same morning Nick began working on the sidewalk, her mother suggested to her father that he go visit.

"She's all alone and has Nina's husband doing the job alone. Just pass by, Tony."

Teresa's father, Tony, didn't have much to do around the house, so he decided to take his wife's suggestion.

* * *

Tony approached his daughter's house.

From the distance, he couldn't make out the face of the man knelt over the wet cement. However, he knew it must have been Nina's husband. After all, this man was only one working.

Tony drew closer, and the face came into view.

"Nick Niceli?"

At the sound of his name, Nick looked up. He recognized Tony as well. But he had no idea of his relationship to Teresa.

"Mr. Tony, what brings you here?"

As an old, tough Sicilian, Tony didn't answer. Instead, he asked a question of his own. "What are you doing here?"

"Oh, I'm doing work for a Sicilian couple."

"Well, that Sicilian couple happens to be my son-in-law Giacomo and my daughter Teresa. They own this house."

Nick's mouth opened, but he didn't have a response. Once again, like a pig, he'd been caught in his own mess.

No other words were exchanged, but Tony was disgusted. This bastard had entered his home with his mistress, acting like she was his girlfriend.

To a Sicilian, if you want to be a pig, go do it far away. Don't you dare bring a mistress into a decent home, especially not acting like an altar boy with a girlfriend. Those things simply weren't done. Otherwise, someone might see and think that decent men like Tony or Carlo condoned this behavior.

Chapter Twenty-Five

As the months passed, Nick's behavior went from bad to worse. His rejection of Nina killed her. It made her feel unworthy of being loved.

Am I so repulsive that not even his manly nature will allow him to surrender? Or can he resist because he's being fed sex elsewhere?

Carlo never asked about their bedroom activities when he called, and Nina wouldn't dare breathe a word to anyone.

However, when her mind was free to roam, this was the thing that consumed her most. She still desired her husband and loved him to the point that she would have forgiven him any sin had he only apologized. But he never did.

"If only the heart worked differently," she'd whisper to herself at night, tears dripping onto her pillow.

Nina believed the heart was ruled by the brain. It reacted with emotions depending on what the brain sent.

You get burned, the brain tells the heart you're burned, and the heart reacts. It screams, feels the pain, and cries out. Or maybe just cries.

Nina's brain put sadness, rejection, and tears into her heart, and it was difficult to let them out.

The real mystery was why her heart and brain seemed so misaligned when it came to her husband.

"My heart wants him, but my brain tells me to spit on him. Maybe I'm going crazy."

* * *

One day around noon, Nick came home. He'd bought three dozen clams and asked if Nina knew how to cook spaghetti with clam sauce.

She was shocked and delighted, in equal parts.

"Of course I do," she said. Without a hint of resentment, she ran to the kitchen at his whim and set about making a delicious meal.

As she set the table, Nick informed her, "I have a friend coming over. Set a place for her too."

Nina obeyed without question. She was in the kitchen still when she heard his friend arrive. She fixed herself to be more presentable, then walked to the dining area.

Nick was all smiles.

"This is Nina," he said as means of introduction. He didn't refer to her as his wife.

Nick's friend was cordial and well-dressed, though not appropriately so for her age. The tight ripped jeans, high heels, and loose ponytail were more suited for a teenager. This woman was well into her forties, over a decade older than Nick.

Nina returned to the kitchen under the guise of checking on her clam sauce. However, she called Teresa. In whispers, she told her neighbor about her husband's new friend.

Teresa arrived a few minutes later.

Nina invited their neighbor to join them for lunch, and soon the four were seated at the table.

Both Teresa and Nina kept their eyes on Nick's friend in the ripped jeans. There was no question what was happening.

Every time Nick spoke, his friend giggled. They exchanged sly glances. She called him *Nick, the sick dick.*

The final red flag was when the friend responded to Nina in perfect Italian. She was from a city near Palermo and spoke the same Sicilian dialect as the rest of them.

Teresa was clever, and nothing got past her radar. She deduced the friend's motives at once. This tramp wanted to start a friendship with Nina because it would make it easier for her to visit Nick.

And that bastard is making his poor, sweet wife be cordial and cook for her! Teresa couldn't believe it.

* * *

Time had softened Nick's fear of his godfather. He'd learned that no matter what disgusting behavior he displayed, Nina wouldn't accuse him. She never went to Carlo.

Nick had more freedom than he'd realized. Soon he fell into an easy pattern.

Once a week, usually on Saturday, he came home for lunch. Afterward, he'd take the kids out. Sometimes, they'd visit the local playground or go on rides at the amusement park.

For Easter, however, he decided to take them to Carmen's house.

The girls were smarter than he realized. Though Lilly was more respectful and closer to her papa, she loved her mother. She had vivid memories of both Carmen and her house, and as she walked up the steps, she immediately understood.

Mamma would not like if it she knew we were here.

Still, Lilly was too polite to refuse. Gina was not.

The little girl stood outside the entire time, refusing to go in. She glared at Carmen with all the hate she could muster.

Trying to win Gina over, Carmen brought out a chocolate Easter bunny. "Here, see? I'm not so bad."

Gina snatched the bunny and flung it onto the floor. The chocolate broke into a million pieces.

"Wow, okay, so you don't like me. I get it!"

"I want my mamma!" Gina bawled.

Nick attempted to calm her with no success. He was forced to put both her and Lilly in the car and drive them home.

Gina was still sobbing when they arrived.

Nina took her daughter at once and cuddled her on her lap. She called Lilly over. Although she wasn't in tears, she seemed equally unnerved.

A few concerned questions made Lilly crack. She whispered the truth to her mother, and rage flashed against the backs of Nina's eyes.

In a voice, soft and sweet, and masking the anger boiling beneath, she reassured Gina. "It's okay, baby. You never have to go there again."

Nina got the girls to her room before turning on her husband. Finally, she screamed at him.

"Lily told me where you took them. How dare you bring my children into that infested house? Did you think my kids were going to become her best friend? Did you think they would like her? That'll never happen, Nick. You're a pig."

* * *

The next day, Nina confided the truth to her friend when she visited Teresa's home. They sent their daughters to play in the basement, and the two women sat around the kitchen table.

Teresa was appalled when Nina finished.

"I never wanted to say it, but he looked like scum from the first day we saw him. Nothing about him gave us good vibes, absolutely nothing. Coming home to you all dressed up, where the hell is he showering and getting dressed? Giacomo and I kept saying."

"Teresa, listen to me," Nina said. "I can't go back to Sicily without a husband, however he treats me here. I have to stay. Nobody sees what he does to me here, just you and Signora Anna. But I can't even run to Signore Carlo because he'll kill Nick."

As Nina spoke, tears began trickling from her eyes.

Teresa soon found herself crying as well.

"Listen Nina, if you have no other choice, I'm here for you one hundred percent. Right now, I don't know what to tell you, but we'll figure something out, *cara mia*."

"This is just what happens in Sicily when a girl gets pregnant. She has to get married to face the town without shame—even if there's no love. I admit, I was wrong. I shouldn't have let him touch me. But you know how persistent a guy can get, and I couldn't resist, and—you know what?" Nina yelled through her tears. "My parents were just as guilty. And the majority of the people in that town. They all think alike."

"Nina, listen to me," Teresa said. "What has happened already happened. You can't dwell on the past. You need to concentrate on the future."

* * *

Months passed with no light in sight, only the same darkness.

Nick was more a bastard than before. The time between his homecomings stretched further. When he did deign to make an appearance, he continued to reject his wife.

Nina's spirt felt crushed every time. It was torture.

Yet, when he called to inform her of his return, she would cook his favorite food, even if it meant barbecuing outside under an umbrella in the middle of a thunderstorm. All she wanted was to please him.

Nick would eat like a rat and after dinner, he'd roll down the sleeves of his shirt, button the cuffs. A few minutes later, he'd be gone, leaving Nina with only a painful knot in her stomach.

Chapter Twenty-Six

In the small town of Bagheria, Nina's daughter Diana was the pride of her grandparents.

Each morning, she woke early to make breakfast. She tidied and cleaned the house. She attended most of the chores, sparing her elderly grandmother the burden. At school, her grades were excellent. About town, she was known as a good girl.

The summer after her mother left with her younger sisters, Diana blossomed from a child to a young lady. She was almost eighteen.

When she resumed school in September, her friends remained the same, but Diana noticed the boys looking at her. She lowered her gaze to avoid making eye contact. Diana was shy and didn't want to acknowledge their stares.

Boys weren't on her mind—not yet.

In mid-November, a new teacher was hired at Diana's high school. His name was Gianni Barella. He was both Diana's homeroom and math teacher.

The girls giggled and whispered about the new handsome, young teacher. Diana didn't pay them much attention.

"He's okay," she said. "No big deal."

* * *

Diana's teachers had always admired her character. She was known for being quiet, humble, and reserved, never letting her emotions get the best of her.

One day, Signor Barella asked her to help him mark some test papers. He trusted her, and she didn't refuse to help.

Impressed by her, he began to call on Diana more often, sometimes without realizing.

The other students, however, took note. It was no secret to them that Diana was Signor Barella's favorite or—as she would've been called in America—the teacher's pet.

* * *

Diana's mornings centered around chores. Once they were finished, she'd wash, groom herself, and head to the place she loved most —school.

"I have a thirst to succeed and learn all I can. Plus, seeing my friends every day is a pleasure," she told her grandparents.

It only increased their pride.

However, it was more than school Diana loved. She didn't know it yet, but soon she would.

Gianni Barella was twenty-three, fresh out of school with a master's degree in education. He was smart, patient, and respectful toward both students and staff.

Plus—as Diana was slowly starting to notice—he was handsome.

It made her a little uncomfortable that he paid her more attention than her classmates, but she didn't think there was anything wrong with it. After all, many of her teachers spoke highly of her.

But Diana wasn't attracted to her other teachers.

One day, a lightbulb went on in her mind.

I have a crush on him, she realized.

That wasn't a big deal. Most of the girls in the school harbored secret feelings for their handsome young teacher.

However, as the weeks passed, Diana's feelings grew stronger.

This wasn't a crush. She was falling in love.

* * *

One Monday morning, Diana was forced to stay home, suffering from severe menstrual cramps.

When Signor Barella noticed her absence, he felt an unexpected sadness. He missed Diana's presence.

What was wrong with him?

The whole day, he tried to get his mind away from his student. When that failed, he focused on the consequences of starting a relationship with her: losing his job, facing legal trouble because she was his student.

Nothing could happen between them.

Without Diana, the day seemed longer and emptier. Signor Barella couldn't concentrate. When three o'clock finally came and the class was dismissed, he took some papers, got in his car, and drove home.

The following morning, he found himself eager to get to school.

"*Buon giorno, Signor Barella*," the assistant principal greeted him when he arrived. She was a young woman, closer to his own age. "You're awfully early this morning."

"I have test papers to mark and a math exam I want to return to the students today."

"Can I get you an espresso?" she offered.

"Yes, please, but with some milk. Strong coffee before breakfast irritates my stomach."

"I have the same problem," she said, a bit too excited to find a commonality. Although older than the students, the assistant principal had developed a similar crush on the handsome new teacher.

Signor Barella turned toward the hallway and walked to his homeroom. He checked his watch to ensure it matched the clock on the wall. It was 7:15, and the school as quiet.

His eyes flicked from his papers to the time, counting down the minutes until his students should arrive. He heard someone walking in the hallway. Instantly, his heart beat faster.

Was it Diana?

Signor Barella's face dropped as the assistant principal arrived with his coffee.

"Here, Signor Barella," she said. "I also brought you a *cornetto* since you said coffee bothers you on an empty stomach."

"That was very thoughtful of you, thank you. How much do I owe you?"

She gave him a flirty smile. "It was my pleasure. You don't owe me a cent."

"You're not only thoughtful, but now you're much too nice."

Beaming, the assistant principal walked away.

If only she knew who had been on his mind all night long.

* * *

The students arrived in twos and threes, but Diana wasn't one of them.

Why isn't she here? What happened to her? Signor Barella's eyes flicked to her empty seat. All the other students were at their desks.

Hiding his sadness, Signor Barella stood to close the door. Before he could, however, a soft voice came from outside.

"Hold on, Signor Barella, let me come in."

It was Diana. She stood before him dressed in a tight pink angora sweater, with a black miniskirt, black tights, and boots. The chill had brought out the pink in her lips and given her cheeks a natural blush. Her long brown hair shone in long waves past her shoulders.

How could Signor Barella not stare?

"Diana, were you hurt? Are you okay? How are you...?" His voice trailed off as he felt his students' eyes on him.

What was he thinking asking so many questions? A teacher didn't display such obvious relief at seeing a student who'd only missed one day.

Signor Barella hurried to cover his mistake.

"I'm so sorry, Diana. I didn't mean to close the door on your foot. I hope I haven't injured you."

Diana stared at her teacher. She knew that the door had been nowhere near her foot. Signor Barella's wide and desperate eyes begged her not to rat him out.

"I'm fine, Signor," Diana assured him. With a smile, she took her seat.

Signor Barella watched her—perhaps a second longer than he should have—before returning to the front of the class. He cleared his throat.

"I never got a chance to grade the test papers yesterday. Can you mark them for me after school today, Diana?" Then, to be safe, he added. "You should choose another of your classmates to help. I really need the results by tonight."

Diana was quick to agree. Signor Barella's lie about hitting her foot coupled with the way he'd stared when he saw her outside had her mind spinning with a wonderous and dangerous idea.

Was it possible her teacher had feelings for her?

* * *

When they'd finished grading the papers, Diana left her friend, Vittoria, in the classroom and went to Signor Barella on her own.

He waited in the staff room. No other teachers remained.

At Diana's entrance, Signor Barella looked up, and for a second, their eyes locked. He kept his smile under control, but his eyes betrayed him, growing wide with infatuation. He stared like a puppy dog whose owner had appeared to give it a treat.

I can't be imagining this, Diana thought.

"You're such a big help to me," Signor Barella said, taking the papers. "I can't thank you enough."

"I don't mind." Diana lingered a second, waiting to see if he'd say more. When he didn't, her shyness returned.

I'm being silly. She chided herself and hurried back to the classroom.

There was no sign of Vittoria. Diana grabbed her bag and coat and hurried outside, hoping to find her. However, her friend had already left.

Did she forget she'd agreed to give me a ride?

To add to the insult, it began to rain, and Diana had neither a ride home nor an umbrella.

This caught the attention of Signor Barella, who'd just stepped outside. With the papers graded, he was ready to leave too, and—if he was being honest—he'd hurried out in the hopes he might catch another glimpse of his student.

He hadn't expected to find her in need of help.

Signor Barella knew it wasn't wise for him to spend too much time alone with this particular student. Then again, why should Diana suffer because of his feelings?

Taking a deep breath, he approached her. "Diana, where is Vittoria? Wasn't she giving you a lift?"

"She must have forgotten," Diana said without a hint of anger or resentment in her voice.

My God, she's so sweet it's killing me, Signor Barella thought. Aloud, he said, "Come. You're here late because of me. The least I can do is drive you home in this rain."

"Really, Signor Barella, it's okay. I've walked plenty of times in bad weather."

"But did anyone offer you a lift then?"

Diana smiled, her heart starting to flutter. "No, not really."

"Then I win this argument. I'm driving you home."

* * *

Neither of them spoke the first five minutes of the drive. Signor Barella didn't know the right words. Diana was too shy.

Finally, Signor Barella found an excuse to break the silence. "Where do you live?" he asked.

"It's the second house from the church on Via Puleo."

"I should have known you lived near the church because you look like an angel." The compliment escaped Signor Barella before he realized.

There was no way to put the words back in his mouth. His face flushed. He thought to himself, *With all the education I have, I really flunked this time.*

"*Grazie, Signor Barella,*" Diana thanked him, shifting in her seat and staring at the floor, too uncomfortable to make eye contact.

"*Prego.*" It was the only response he could muster.

Silence crept in again. Signor Barella turned on the radio, hoping it would break the awkwardness. The song "*Sempre Ti Amo*" played. It was a song for lovers.

This was too much. Signor Barella burst out laughing.

Bewildered, Diana turned to him. "What's so funny?"

"You think someone set this up?"

"I don't know what you mean," Diana said. Secretly, however, she wondered if she did.

Signor Barella stopped the car on the busy avenue. It seemed safer than going to a discreet location. He didn't want this getting out of hand.

"Listen, Diana." Signor Barella turned to her. "You and I both know what's happening here. Are you feeling the same way I am?"

Diana's cheeks flushed. She hoped they were, but she'd have been mortified if she answered *yes* only to discover that her teacher was talking about something different.

"I don't know what you mean," she said again.

"I know it's considered wrong for a teacher to fall in love with his student, but my heart only thinks of you. How can I control my heart?" He sounded so desperate.

"Don't," Diana replied quickly, "because I feel the same way."

Her admission didn't surprise Signor Barella the way his had shocked Diana. However, hearing it delighted the teacher all the same—until the reality of their situation knocked the excitement from him.

"This is harder than the exam I took for my master's degree." He sighed and took Diana's hand. He squeezed it tight and kissed it. "We have to be discreet. No one can know how we feel. But, while I'm being courageous, let me make it clear—I love you, Diana. I've known it for a while but was afraid to say."

"Me too." Diana's heart pounded. Her skin tingled from where his lips had pressed against her hand. She couldn't believe her good fortune.

Or was it ill?

"Signor Barella, are you going to get in trouble because of me? I don't want anything bad to happen to you."

"*Non ti preoccupare, dolcezza mia,*" he hurried to reassure her. "We just can't make our love known."

"I can keep it a secret. I'd never put you in danger, Signor Barella."

The teacher smiled. "Diana, please, when we're in private, call me Gianni."

Chapter Twenty-Seven

Diana's grandfather waited outside with an umbrella, hoping to see her walking home.

Signor Barella's car stopped near the house. Diana climbed from the passenger seat.

Her grandfather lowered his head, trying to see who was driving.

Diana didn't attempt to hide it.

"*Nonno*, this is my teacher," she explained. "I had to stay late at school grading papers with a friend. When it started to rain, he kindly offered to drive us."

What a considerate and thoughtful teacher, Diana's grandfather thought. He assumed that Signor Barella had driven both students home and even thanked him for his kindness before putting the umbrella over his granddaughter and walking her home.

"*Pupa mia!*" Diana's grandmother greeted her when she walked in. "You're nice and dry. Did you have an umbrella?"

"No, *Nonna*, I got a ride from the teacher who we were helping."

"Ahh, *che bravo maestro!*" Diana's grandmother praised Signor Barella. Much like her husband, the old woman missed the red flags.

* * *

For Diana, this experience was new. Signor Barella was her first crush, her first love, and her first relationship.

Due to the age gap, her teacher had more experience. Years ago, Gianni Barella had fallen in love with a girl who'd betrayed him with his best friend. He'd cut her out of his life without regret and moved to Palermo to start a new life as a teacher.

Gianni came from a wealthy family. When he made this change, his parents bought a beautiful villa in a town near Bagheria. He lived there with them as was common in Italy for an unmarried young man.

Despite sharing a home with his parents, Gianni enjoyed a good deal of privacy. He lived on the second story of the villa and spent most of his time sitting on his balcony, overlooking the blue water of Santa Elia. Only when diner was served did he descend and spend time with his parents.

That same afternoon, after dropping Diana at her grandparents' house, Gianni raced home. Out of respect, he announced his presence with a shout, "*Ciao Mamma, sono a casa!*" Then, he raced up the stairs, jumping two steps at a time.

Wearing a huge smile, he flung open the door, threw himself onto the couch, and stared at the ceiling.

I told her I love her. And she loves me too.

Gianni couldn't wait to get to work tomorrow.

* * *

The next day, Diana was running late for school.

She kept making a mess of her chores. The eggs burned. The mop spread the bits of mud instead of cleaning them. She dropped a glass.

"*Nonna*, what is wrong with me this morning?" Diana asked, hurrying to get the broom.

Her poor grandmother didn't have a clue. But the answer was obvious: she was in love. All her thoughts revolved around her teacher. How could she focus on what she was doing?

Finally, she cleared the broken glass. "*Ciao, Nonna.* I'll see you at three."

"*Ciao, amore mio,*" her grandmother called endearingly. "Be careful, and don't talk to strangers."

Little did the old woman know, it wasn't strangers that she had to fear.

* * *

Diana ran up the flight of steps and found the classroom door already closed.

Oh no!

The doors locked from the inside for security reasons. Diana felt embarrassed to knock—arriving late always drew unwanted attention—but there was no other way to get in.

Diana raised her hand and tapped lightly.

Signor Barella opened it.

"*Ciao, Diana.* You know you're late." His voice was cool and casual.

Diana stared at him, heart beating madly in her chest. How could he be so calm when just the sight of him had her giddy?

Signor Barella called her in and walked to his desk.

He ignored her the entire time they were in homeroom. She avoided looking at him too.

It wasn't until later that they managed to be alone.

* * *

Diana had a math class with Signor Barella that afternoon.

This time, she made sure she was the first one to arrive.

Gianni's eyes met hers the moment she stepped into the classroom. His lips spread into a huge smile.

Diana's heart fluttered again. "Oh God," she admitted, approaching his desk. "How I wanted to see you this morning and couldn't even say a proper hello."

"Listen, Diana, can you bring these books to the library?" He tapped a stack on the edge of his desk. Then pulled something shiny from his pocket. "Here are the keys."

Diana held out her hand. "The library isn't locked."

"It's for the wall closet." He pressed the key into her palm.

Uncertain, Diana carried the books to the library. She unlocked the door to the closet and began packing the books within. As she rested the last one down, she felt him behind her.

Gianni turned her toward him and kissed her passionately.

It was the perfect kiss.

His lips pressed softly against hers. Diana felt like she was on a roller coaster, unable to catch her breath—her first kiss! It was intoxicating and delightful.

She'd never experienced anything like this before, and it wasn't a boy who held Diana in his arms, but a man. Signor Barella was now teaching her the art of lovemaking.

After a long first kiss, he gave her a quick one, then rushed out of the library.

Diana followed five minutes later.

* * *

Signor Barella asked Diana and Vittoria to stay after school again to help him grade homework.

When the dismissal bell rang, most of the students hurried to their next class. However, Vittoria walked to his desk.

"I'm sorry, Signor Barella, I can't stay," she said. "I have a dentist appointment this afternoon and have to leave school early."

As her homeroom teacher, Signor Barella had already made a note of this in his attendance. However, he pretended to be surprised.

"Fine, I understand, Vittoria. I'll see who else I can ask to stay and help me."

Of course, Signor Barella did no such thing.

* * *

"*Amore mio!*" Gianni shouted as he entered his classroom.

Diana looked up from the desk. She pressed her index finger to her lips. "Shhh, someone will hear you."

"Don't worry, my love. No one is here." Gianni had waited in the main office for the staff to leave. He'd even promised them that he'd lock the doors. "I've got you all to myself."

"Oh, you're so bad." Diana giggled. "I didn't know this side of you."

"And you're so damn adorable and innocent." Gianni walked slowly toward her, wrapped her in his arms and started kissing her without pity.

Diana didn't resist.

On instinct, she kissed him back, responding to him with a shy enthusiasm that thrilled Gianni. It made him hungry for her.

If they had been interrupted, who knows what might have happened.

A knock came on the door.

At once, Gianni and Diana flew apart. She sat at the desk, pen in hand, staring at the papers as though she'd been grading them. He grabbed the phone and lifted it from the receiver before going to the door.

The janitor stood outside. He needed to clean the classroom.

Gianni could have slapped himself. He'd made sure the other teachers and office staff were gone, but he'd forgotten about the janitor.

Careful not to arouse suspicion, Gianni went to the phone, pretending that he'd just stepped away from a call.

"I'm back, Vittoria," he said, speaking to the beeping dial tone. "Yes, I understand. I'm sorry you were in such pain. You did the right thing calling your mother to pick you up. Don't worry about the papers. Diana can finish them tomorrow."

Then, just in case the janitor hadn't been eavesdropping, Gianni turned to Diana and explained loudly, "Poor Vittoria was in pain with her tooth. When she went to the bathroom, she called her mother, and she came to pick her up."

He wanted to ensure that the janitor thought another child had been there with Diana.

"I'm sorry, Signor Barella," the janitor said. "I didn't know you were still in the building."

"It's okay. I did mention to the office that I would be staying here for an hour or so to catch up on the students' exams."

"Well, this is my last classroom. I'm leaving soon."

"So are we," Gianni said, expression more relaxed than he felt. "Do you mind locking up? The other child just went home with a bad toothache, and we can finish tomorrow."

"Yes, of course," the janitor agreed.

"I'll drive the student home," Gianni said. Then, to avoid suspicion, he added, "I know her grandfather."

* * *

Diana stared at him in amazement as she climbed into his car. "Boy, you're good."

"Well, I do know your grandfather, don't I?"

"Yeah, but you only met him once, and you made him think you guys were buddies." She giggled, then whispered three more words: "I love you."

While driving, Gianni took her hand, brought it to his mouth and caressed it gently on his lips. The kiss that followed was sweet.

This time, he found a discreet, empty street to stop the car.

Gianni wrapped his arm around Diana, pulling her toward him. He kissed her with deep desire. She was intoxicating. He couldn't get enough. Gently, he started to caress her breast.

Then, suddenly, a face pressed to the window—the assistant principal.

Gianni pulled back in horror. Dianna covered her face with her hair.

The assistant principal stepped back. Too embarrassed to confront him, she principal hurried away. What did she care who Gianni kissed. She had no claim. He wasn't hers.

Gianni leaned back in his seat. His eyes widened with panic as he watched her leave. "Of all the people in this town, did it have to be her?"

"Don't worry," Diana reassured him. "She didn't see my face. I realized she was there and hid behind my hair."

"*Sie una brava student, amore mio,*" Gianni complimented Diana. "If she brings this issue to the school, I'll tell them that what I do after hours is none of their business and embarrass her for being a snitch and a blabbermouth."

Gianni kissed Diana again, harder and longer. Against his will, he had to stop, however, to drive her home. Otherwise, he'd have to deal with her grandparents.

* * *

Diana stepped out the car, feeling as though she were floating on a cloud. Gianni gave her one last look of longing before taking off.

Neither realized that they'd been followed.

"*Dove sei strata, cuore mio?*" Diana's grandmother asked where she'd been as she came into the house. "Again, you had to grade papers for that teacher?"

"*Si, Nonna,*" Diana replied.

"I hope he appreciates what you do for him," her grandmother said.

Diana grinned secretly with pleasure. "I believe he does."

Chapter Twenty-Eight

Thursday morning was cloudy, and as the day progressed, it grew darker. This gloom had nothing to do with the weather, but everything to do with Signor Gianni Barella.

After witnessing him kissing a brunette in his car, the assistant principal had grown curious. She'd followed him, only to see Diana Niceli exit the vehicle and enter her grandparents' house.

At the start of the school day, she'd gone straight to the principal. She claimed to have witnessed Diana embracing Signor Barella, possibly engaging in sexual activity.

The school had a zero-tolerance policy for sexual behavior or physical contact that could lead to sexual activity between a teacher and a student.

The principal summoned Signor Barella and fired him at once. There would be no chance for the teacher to plead his case before the school board. Instead, the authorities were called.

* * *

Diana entered the classroom, expecting to see her love. But Signor Barella was missing.

Where is he? Diana wondered. It never occurred to her that he was downstairs in the principal's office waiting for the authorities to arrive.

Diana watched the clock on the wall. Class should have started.

The door opened. A jolt of excitement shot through Diana. She turned, expecting to see Gianni.

It was the principal.

"Signor Barella is no longer employed here," he informed the class. "A new teacher will be substituting for the necessary time."

Diana clasped her chest. It felt as though a sword had been plunged through her heart.

This reaction confirmed the principal's suspicions. "Diana Niceli, I'll need you to come with me to my office."

A hushed whisper spread amongst the class. Was Diana in trouble or was she needed to assist with more paperwork?

Diana followed the principal to his office. As she entered, she saw Signor Barella, hands cuffed behind the chair. Standing beside him were the deputy captain *carabiniere* and the assistant principal.

Gianni's eyes met Diana's own. He stared at her with such a tender, loving expression that her heart broke.

"Why is he in handcuffs?" she demanded. However, given the people in the room and the expression on the principal's face, it was easy for her to guess what had happened. "He did nothing wrong. What crime is it to fall in love? Our relationship is not dirty. It's not based on sex, but pure, clean love."

The assistant principal snorted softly.

Diana turned her glare to the older woman. "Did you do all this because he never gave you the time of day? Did you feel rejected? Is that why you've lied to the authorities?"

The assistant principal felt her face grow hot. She opened her mouth but couldn't find a defense. How had a student known about her crush?

"Diana, I beg of you, calm down," Gianni pleaded from his seat. "Please, I don't want to see you upset. Everything will be okay." He turned to the deputy captain *carabiniere*. "Can I please make a phone call to my father?"

The deputy captain was only following the school's protocol. The young teacher had done nothing wrong in his opinion. This made him more lenient. "I'll give you the phone, but please, just one phone call, Signor Barella."

Crying uncontrollably, Diana took a seat beside her teacher. Gianni tried to console her as the deputy captain undid the cuffs. She tried to compose herself for his sake.

The moment he had the phone, Gianni called his father.

"Papa, I've been arrested," he said. "I have no time to explain. Come to the school as quickly as possible and bring your lawyer."

* * *

It was approaching noon by the time Gianni's father arrived with the lawyer. Diana remained in the office alongside her teacher for the entire morning as they waited.

The lawyer conferred with Gianni in private before coming to speak to the deputy captain and the principal.

"There was no force of sexuality because sex did not occur, nor was there any inappropriate conduct inside or outside of school. He's been accused by a coworker who has no proof or evidence to support her claim. All she saw was a teacher driving home a student with an impeccable record and reputation."

This defense was enough for the deputy captain. He released Signor Barella from the handcuffs.

* * *

Diana left school early that day. She found Signor Barella waiting for her outside.

The first thing he did was pull her into a hug. She wrapped her arms around his neck and sobbed against his chest.

He cradled her like a baby. "Why are you still crying, *amore*?"

Diana couldn't put her sadness into words. It wasn't only the ordeal with her teacher. The day's events had made her miss her mother and father. She loved her elderly grandparents, but they knew nothing of what she was going through.

Gianni wiped her tears, kissing her cheeks as he did so. "*Amore*, I want to go to your *nonno* and ask for your hand in marriage. Would you like that? My parents can also come to the house and ask him."

Diana blinked tears from her eyes. Her heart felt ready to burst. She stared up at him. "What are you saying?"

"You didn't think I only wanted you part time, did you? I want you forever. I want you to be the mother of my children. I want to grow old with you, to spend every day of my life near you, to wake up in your bed. I want you. Period."

The tears spilled from Diana's eyes again. She burrowed her face against his chest, feeling protected and desired. "*Ti amo, Gianni.*"

* * *

While Diana phoned her grandparents and invented a lie about staying late to grade papers once again, Gianni called his mother, Caterina.

"I'm bringing home a girl. I want to introduce her to you."

"Of course, *figlio mio*," she said. "Any friend of yours is also a friend of mine."

Gianni chuckled. "Mamma, I think she is more than a friend. But if that's how we define this, I hope to make her a friend for life."

* * *

Both of Gianni's parents took an immediate liking to Diana. She was a good girl with a respectful attitude.

"Come sit with me," Caterina called to Diana to join her on the couch in their living room.

Diana sat shyly on the edge of the cushion. "You have a beautiful home, Signora Caterina."

"*Grazie, Diana.*"

"I love the paintings. You have excellent taste."

Caterina smiled. "I can't take the credit. The interior decorator chose all the wall décor. I just selected the colors and the furniture. Though Gianni chose a lot of the outdoor décor, even the shape of the pool."

"I didn't know you had an outdoor pool."

"Come, let me show you the rest of the villa. After all, it was Gianni's doing. He consulted closely with the architect."

Caterina took Diana's hand and led her outside to the veranda. From there, they could see the pool below, shaped like a figure eight. Along the edge, a pair of large porcelain pots overflowed with flowers and greenery. They caught Diana's eye at once.

"Do you like the planters?" Caterina asked. "They're my favorites in the entire villa. They're antiques. I don't know how many hundreds of years old, but they were found in an abandoned castle in Verona. Who knows, they might have belonged to Romeo or Juliet."

Caterina laughed, and Diana offered her a shy smile.

"See the circular balcony above us?" Caterina asked, pointing upward. "That's part of Gianni's quarters. He lives upstairs but loves having his privacy."

She then led Diana past a large mosaic table in the center of the veranda toward another circular balcony. From there, they had a perfect view of the blue sea of Santa Elia.

"The water's so clear," Diana said with amazement.

"That's because it's not a fisherman's path. It only accommodates luxury yachts and sailboats," Caterina informed her. "When we first bought the villa, the rocks made it impossible for us to get to the water, so my husband had a contractor build forty cement steps. They lead to a private beach area, just for us."

With each new thing she was shown, Diana grew increasingly amazed. *Wow,* she thought, *it's nice to have money.*

A housekeeper and cook prepared refreshments for them. Caterina invited Diana to stay for dinner, but the young girl politely declined.

"*Grazie,* but my grandparents are expecting me soon. Maybe another time."

"*Brava, Diana, mi fa piacere,*" Caterina complimented her. "You have a lot of respect for your grandparents. I like that about you."

These words thrilled Gianni, who was watching from a few feet away. He'd hoped his mother would approve of Diana. It made him more confident in his decision.

* * *

"*Amore mio*," Diana said. "I'm sorry I can't invite you in. I need time to tell my grandparents. They think that you're just my nice teacher. Please tell me you understand?"

"Of course I do, and I respect that," Gianni assured her. "Don't worry, when the time is right it will happen."

He stopped the car a few feet from her house. He leaned over and gave her a steamy, passionate kiss, followed by five quick ones.

As she stepped out, Gianni shouted after her, "I want you, Diana!"

She giggled and leaned back through the window to kiss him one last time. When she pulled away, he extended his left arm, playing as if to grab her.

"I miss you already," he said.

At that moment, Diana's grandfather walked out.

She spun to Gianni and widened her eyes, alerting him to her *nonno's* presence.

Quickly, the former teacher pulled his arm back, shifted into first gear, and sped off.

Diana smiled at her grandfather. "*Ciao, Nonno.* My teacher just drove me home, but he was in a hurry to drop my friend next. But he did say to tell you hello."

"*Ma che bravo stu maestro*,' her grandfather said. He'd have reconsidered his compliment if he had any idea what Signor Barella was planning.

* * *

The police weren't pressing charges against Gianni. He could have fought with the school to reclaim his job. In his estimation, his dismissal had been unfair, but he had no interest in returning.

I'll find many other jobs in Palermo, he assured himself. *I'm in no hurry.*

Besides, as important as his career was, it paled in comparison to Diana's love.

This was why, the following morning, Gianni rushed from his house, leaving before his parents had even arisen. He had one thought in mind.

He needed to see Diana before she got to school.

Gianni waited by the bus stop. The minute she stepped onto the sidewalk, he ran from his car and called out her name.

Diana heard. Instead of walking toward her school, she turned in the opposite direction and went toward him.

"*Amore*, how I missed you," Gianni told her, pulling her into a hug once more. "Last night, I went to bed early with you on my mind. How I desired to have you in my arms. I'm dying, Diana. I want you so badly, it's killing me."

She climbed into the car beside him. The rain started to pour. There was no one out on the streets and only a few other vehicles passed by.

Diana felt safe to throw her arms around his neck and whisper, "I want you too, Gianni. I desire your kisses, your touches, your voice telling me that you love me. It's hard for me too, Gianni. Last night, I cried and asked God why I couldn't be near you."

"Please, don't say another word. It's hard enough dealing with my thoughts. Hearing you talk to me that way makes it a hundred times more difficult." Gianni cupped her face in his hands, holding her still. Then, he kissed her hard, with such desire and passion that it surprised even him. His hand slid from her cheek to her breast.

Gently, she moved it away.

"Why, Diana? I love you," he said.

"I know," she whispered, "but do you realize where we are? The school is up the street. Can you imagine if we get caught again? Even if you're not my teacher anymore, you once were. What will people think?"

*　*　*

In the days and weeks to come, Gianni had to be satisfied with only spending time together in his car. He drove further away from Bagheria so Diana wouldn't be recognized. She never refused his invitations.

One morning, he met her again before school at the same bus stop. After Diana climbed into his car, Gianni drove off. He had a plan she didn't know about.

"*Amore,* where are you taking me?" she asked. "We've gone too far from the school."

He looked at her. "Do you trust me?"

"Of course I do. I trust you with my life."

Gianni cleared his throat. "*Amore,* although we've known each other for only a few months, I feel I've known you for a lifetime."

Diana smiled. She felt the same way. But she had no idea what her former teacher was about to suggest.

"Marry me today, Diana."

"What?"

"Marry me right now."

She stared at him, unable to believe what she'd heard. "*Ma che dice?*"

"I said let's elope, Diana. Now, today."

She laughed, thinking he was joking. However, his expression said otherwise. "You're serious, aren't you?"

"I've never been more serious in my entire life, *amore mio.*" Gianni's voice trembled with conviction.

Diana stared at him. She could hardly believe it. "I don't have a change of clothes, just what I'm wearing."

"Is that your problem, *amore mio*? I'll buy you all the best clothes in Italy. You don't even have to ask."

Diana's heart pounded in her chest. She gripped her seat, mind spinning. "Oh my God, Gianni, I'm scared."

"Of who?"

"My poor *Nonna e Nonno.* They'll be expecting me back at three."

"We'll call them before then."

"Wait, Gianni, please. Give me some time."

"*Amore,* if you don't want to marry me, I'll try to understand. I don't want to force you. But if we don't do this now, you need to get to school soon. Otherwise, we'll have the authorities looking for you. *Che dice?*"

"Please, drive me back to school. Please, don't be mad. I can't just run away like this."

"It's okay, *amore.*" Gianni sighed with great disappointment. "I still love you and respect your decision. But please, try to understand for me too. I'm dying to have you as my wife, my lover, my companion for life."

FRANCESCA FALLETTA MARCECA

"Oh Gianni, why must everything be so complicated?"

Chapter Twenty-Nine

True to his word, Gianni turned the car around and drove Diana to school.

Hearing his desire for her but still having her wishes respected made her faith in him grow even stronger. For the first time, Diana confided in him about her parents, what her mother had endured and why she'd gone to America.

"I never said a word to anyone, but I trust you," Diana said, twisting a strand of hair around her finger. "When Mamma left, I didn't want to remain in Sicily. As much as I love Bagheria and my grandparents, I wanted to stay with my mother and sisters. But I knew it would be easier for her if I stayed here, so I pretended to be happy about the decision. She was going through so much, I didn't want to add to her problems, so I hid my tears from her. My father has no idea what he's put our family through—my mother especially. That's part of why I asked you to bring me back. Mamma has been hurt so much. How will she feel if she learns I've eloped?"

"I'm so very sorry for what you've been going through," Gianni said, squeezing her knee after she'd finished. "But you can't stop life, Diana. It won't erase what's been done."

Tears welled in her eyes.

Gianni hurried to continue, "Did you ever think your mom will be happy that you've found true love, a love that will last longer than forever? I read once that something good will always come out of a bad situation. Sometimes, I think God sees a family having a really bad time, so he sends some good into their lives. Besides, she's going to love me—her daughter does!"

Diana wiped the few tears that had fallen, a smile replaced her sadness. "Thank you, Gianni, for coming to Bagheria, but mostly thank you for coming into my life."

* * *

As Diana walked into the school building, tears streamed down her face. Should she have insisted Gianni take her back to school? She felt so confused.

More than ever, she missed her mother.

Diana recalled the joy she'd felt spending time with her family. She wished she could hear her sister's laughter. She even missed fiery little Gina attempting to boss her around.

Class was about to begin. Diana wiped her face and slid into her seat. The new substitute stood at the front.

Diana couldn't focus on the teacher. Gianni's words repeated in her mind: *You can't stop your life, Diana. It won't erase what's been done.*

He was right. She couldn't erase her father's wrongdoings. Diana had her own future to think about.

Hopefully, it would include Gianni.

* * *

That Friday night, overwhelmed with the decision she had to make, Diana crawled into bed. She found it impossible to sleep. Thoughts of her parents and Gianni battled in her mind.

Her mother had eloped with her father. Look how that had turned out.

But they had no choice. Mamma was pregnant.

Diana flung herself out of bed, opened her closet, and grabbed a suitcase. She'd made up her mind. She would elope with Gianni before she became pregnant. No one in the village would whisper about her. Diana was still a virgin and proud of it. Her situation was nothing like her parents.

How do I tell Gianni I'm ready to elope?

Diana's head felt light and giddy. She tried out different phrases as she packed.

"I'm ready to marry you. Or is that too on the nose? My God, what's the best way to say it? I want to wake up next to you every morning. Yes, that's it. That's how I feel."

A smile spread across Diana's face.

* * *

Diana had already planned to spend Saturday with Gianni. She'd informed her grandparents that she needed to do research for a school report. The most up-to-date encyclopedias were at the library in Palermo. They assumed she was heading there when she left the house.

Gianni waited for her at the bus stop as usual.

When Diana stepped off, she looked more beautiful than ever—tall, slim, with the grace of a super model. Gianni lost himself in her enchanting eyes and pink lips, especially when they broke into a radiant smile.

He never even noticed that she was holding a suitcase.

Diana quickly placed her bag in the trunk before climbing into the car.

"Hello, Gianni," she said.

He leaned in, kissed her, then whispered in her ear, "*Sempre ti amo.*" When Gianni turned on his cassette player, the car filled with their song.

"Oh Gianni, you're so special!" Diana exclaimed. She kissed him deeply without a care in the world.

He surrendered to the moment, indulging in the kiss as she melted against him.

After they broke apart, his fingers brushed the hair from her neck, sending chills down her spine. He held her hands gently, yet firmly in front of her. Diana felt safe.

Gianni kissed her shoulder, trailing his lips along her skin toward her ear. He nibbled gently on the lobe.

It ignited her desire even more.

Gianni pulled his face back, locking his eyes with hers. He smiled. Then, he guided her right hand to rest against his heart, holding it there. His eyes radiated love, protection, and respect.

Diana smiled. She couldn't believe how much she loved the man before her.

Gianni released her hand and guided her face closer so that it rested against his chest. He wrapped his arm around her.

In that moment, Dianna hoped he would never let go.

"I have a surprise for you," Gianni whispered in her ear.

Diana grinned. "I have one for you too."

* * *

They drove to Palermo, a lively city bustling with people. Diana had no idea what he had planned until he parked and led her into a jewelry boutique.

"Behold, Florentino Finest Luxury Jewelry," Gianni said.

"Oh my God!" Diana couldn't believe it. She'd heard of the place. It was the finest in the city, but she'd never visited herself.

"This is my mother's favorite store," Gianni informed her. "Just yesterday, she told me, *if you're serious about Diana, make sure to go to Florentino.*"

The workers had been expecting Gianni Barella to arrive. They escorted him and Diana to a private office where they sat behind a desk. A man entered with a suitcase filled with engagement rings.

Diana covered her mouth, overcome with emotion. "Oh Gianni, you didn't have to do this. I would have accepted a simple handkerchief as a token of our love."

"Come, *amore mio*, let's see if we choose the same one," he said.

Diana's eyes landed on a stunning ring, but she hesitated to voice her preference. It featured twenty-four smaller stones set in a square around a large two-karat diamond. The gems sparkled like a million stars. This piece was too brilliant for Diana to even dream of owning.

Gianni watched her, noticing her reaction. He could tell which one she loved best even though she hadn't said it.

Of course, she's too modest to admit that she likes the most elaborate one.

What Diana didn't realize was that he'd already had that ring custom designed for her. The others were merely distractions.

"I've already paid for the one you like," Gianni whispered, pointing to it.

Diana was speechless and overcome with joy as she watched the beautiful ring being wrapped in the store's signature packaging.

As they left, the workers congratulated them on their engagement and wished Gianni well. All of them seemed to know his name.

"Have you bought other gifts here before?" Diana asked, unable to help her curiosity.

Gianni chuckled. "I've certainly visited plenty of times."

"Oh." An unfamiliar stab of jealousy shot through Diana. Her former teacher was older. How many other women had he treated to fine pieces of jewelry.

The emotion was obvious on her face.

Gianni smiled, stopping beside his car and turning to her. "You're jealous. Please, ask me why I've been so many times."

"Okay, why?" Diana asked.

Gianni laughed again. He couldn't help it. Her jealousy was endearing. "You're not very observant today, *amore mio*."

Diana's brow furrowed. "You're talking like a teacher. Who talks like that to the girl he loves?"

They both laughed, but Gianni did clarify, "When we first entered, I mentioned that my mother loves this store. I've accompanied her here many times. *Comprende, amore mio?*"

"You did say that. Yes, that makes sense," Diana admitted. "I'm sorry. I was wondering if you'd purchased other engagement rings here."

Gianni's hearty laugh filled the air.

* * *

Gianni took Diana on a tour of the city, visiting the Cathedral of Palermo and several historic sites. She loved every moment. From there, he drove them to Villa Francese, a luxurious five-star hotel and resort with an exclusive restaurant. He'd made dinner reservations. The day's perfect temperature allowed them to dine outdoors *al fresco*.

A beautiful table had been prepared for them on the patio. It overlooked the beautiful water of Mondello.

This is the most enchanting day, Diana thought.

After finishing dinner and enjoying champagne and dessert, they got it the car. Gianni was ready to drive back to Bagheria. He started the car.

They'd gone only a short distance when Diana took his hand from the steering wheel, holding it in her own.

"What's up, *amore mio*?" Gianni asked, sensing her anticipation.

Diana took a deep breath. Unable to suppress her smile, she asked, "So, what time are we waking up tomorrow?"

Gianni's head tilted. "What are you saying?"

"Marry me, Gianni Barella. Marry me now. Tonight."

"What are you talking about?"

"Let's elope, Gianni. Right now, at this very moment. I'm ready to live the rest of my life with you. I want to wake up next to you every morning in bed."

"Oh my God!" Gianni could scarcely believe it. Shock, joy, and love poured out in his words. "Oh my God! How I adore you, Diana Niceli! Wow!" Then, something caught his attention. "I hope you don't want to stop home for your clothes."

"Nope. They're in the trunk of your car. I put my suitcase in this morning."

"And I didn't notice?"

Diana smiled mischievously. "Perhaps you're the one who's not so observant."

Gianni laughed. Swiftly, he made a U-turn and sped back toward Villa Francese.

"What about your clothes?" Diana inquired.

"Oh, I've got a pair of pants and a pair of underwear."

"Great! Where are they?"

"On me! I'm wearing them." Gianni laughed.

The sound was infectious. Diana joined in, laughing until her sides hurt.

* * *

When they returned to Villa Francese, Gianni booked them a hotel room for the next ten days, and soon they were upstairs.

Diana sat by the desk in their luxury suite. Her eyes were glued to the phone. Difficult as it was, she needed to call her *nonna*. Otherwise, her grandparents would spend the night worrying.

I won't reveal too much information—just that I've eloped with my teacher who Nonno met.

Diana took a deep breath and lifted the phone.

Her grandmother answered. In a rush, she repeated the line as she'd planned. Then, added, "He loves me, and I love him too. We're very happy. I'm okay, and I'll call you tomorrow. Please don't ask too many questions. I love you, *Nonna*."

With that, Diana hung up.

Her heart pounded in her chest. With the stress of informing her grandparents gone, she had nothing to distract her from what lay ahead.

Gianni was in the bathroom, taking a quick shower. Diana stared at the door, waiting for him to return. *I hope he doesn't come out naked.*

Gianni didn't. Aware of his bride's innocence, he emerged with a towel wrapped around his body. However, his clothes were folded on the chair.

"Hold on. I'd like a quick shower too," Diana said, leaping from the chair.

"But you're so clean, my love."

"I still want to refresh before I give all of myself to you."

"Okay. Please hurry," he urged.

She smiled at him and whispered, "I will."

Inside the bathroom, she took a fast shower, dried off, and opened her suitcase. She pulled out a two-piece white bridal negligee made of silk. Her mother had purchased and saved it for her—though Nina hadn't anticipated her daughter having need of it so soon.

The negligee was mostly transparent with lace imported from Spain around the collar and the edges of the long coat. It accentuated Diana's curves and felt as soft as butter. She adjusted the sleeves, brushed her long, wet hair neatly from her face, and stepped into the bedroom.

At the sight of her, all of Gianni's senses came alive.

He felt as though he was staring at an angel, captivating and divine.

She approached him on the bed.

Her scent—fresh and clean, and almost delicate—enraptured him. Yet it was nothing compared to her voice, soft and shy, whispering "I'm yours, Gianni. Take me."

Gianni rose slowly, walking to where she stood. His fingers trailed along her back as he kissed her softly. She didn't shy away.

He leaned back so he could drink in the sight of her again. With his index finger, he outlined her soft, wet lips.

This time, when he kissed her, he didn't pull away. His towel and her negligee dropped to the floor.

Chapter Thirty

Lilly was also attending school. On Teresa's advice, Nina had registered her middle daughter at Saint Bernadette Catholic School in Dyker Heights. Teresa had two children of her own who attended as well. Through their mothers' friendship, they'd grown close to both of Nina's daughters. Lilly was particularly close with Teresa's daughter, Danielle. The two were thrilled to attend the same school.

Nina was pleased as well. For her, Saint Bernadette was a beacon of normalcy in their otherwise tense situation.

Early one cold morning, while waiting in the yard for the school day to begin, Nina met another Sicilian woman. Her name was Adriana. She had a child in Lilly's class.

On this particular day, Adriana was accompanied by her mother, Agata. The old woman wore black clothing, with her hair pinned in a tight bun and covered with a black handkerchief. To other Sicilians, her attire was a clear signal that she was in mourning. Her eyes watched everything with hawkish observance, but she seldom spoke.

There was an eerie quality to Agata. Her gaze sent chills up Nina's spine. However, Adriana was warmer.

Over time, Nina chatted with the two, and grew to like Adriana. Still, she was hesitant to reveal too much, uncertain how Agata would respond. All Nina revealed was that she had a husband who worked out of state and returned home weekly (though, in truth, it was closer to monthly now.)

One day, Agata didn't accompany her daughter to school.

Feeling bolder, Nina invited her fellow Sicilian over for coffee. Adriana accepted.

The two walked to Nina's house together and started chatting. Immediately, they hit it off, and soon were giggling over how much they had in common. They shared stories of Sicily and found they were a similar age and had the same longing for their homeland.

Soon, Adriana became Nina's true friend.

As the two spent more time together, Nina grew increasingly comfortable. Even Agata no longer spooked her.

One morning, after the children had gone into school and only the three of them remained near the gate, Nina decided to open up about her situation with Nick.

To her surprise, Adriana had experienced something similar.

"What did you do?" Nina asked her.

"I got a good lawyer, and I divorced him," Adriana said. She was more Americanized, more educated, and had more support in the country than poor Nina. After her husband proved to be a severe narcissist, Adriana had managed to divorce him for physical and mental abuse, cruelty, and constant infidelity. The court had made sure he was still paying for his behavior.

Agata, on the other hand, was not Americanized. She'd grown up in the 1930s in Sicily when high school wasn't mandatory. Her opinion of Nina's situation was different.

Another morning, when Adriana had stepped away to deal with her child, Agata whispered to Nina, "You should woo your husband back to you."

Adriana, well aware of her mother's limited education and outdated beliefs, had always ignored the old woman's suggestions. Had she been present, she might have stopped Agata from saying more.

Nina, however, was intrigued.

"How?" she asked, drawing closer so she could hear the old woman's soft voice.

Agata believed in old folk magic, which had once been practiced in the dense, wooded mountains of southern Sicily. In her usual whisper, she shared some of the secrets with Nina.

"The blood from your menstrual period will bond with his blood, making him desire to be near you, to yearn for you, and want you."

This might sound absurd, but with only a limited education herself—she'd never reached beyond the sixth grade—Nina was gullible enough to believe Agata's words.

"There is a spell..." the old woman said. Her voice trailed off, waiting to see if more information would be requested.

Unlike Adriana, Nina had no money for lawyers. She didn't even have access to Nick's financial information. In the eyes of the law, she was an illegal immigrant, with no rights. Although she had Signora Anna and Teresa, her family were back in Sicily. Nina had nothing to fall back on.

It cannot get darker than midnight, she thought. It was an old Italian proverb that meant her situation couldn't get any worse.

With nothing to lose, Nina asked the old woman for the instructions.

According to Agata, Nina had to retrieve her menstrual blood from a tampon or cloth pad and squeeze it out onto a small ceramic saucer. Once it dried, she was to pulverize it with the back of a wooden spoon. Then, the blood could be dissolved in hot liquids, like tea, coffee or soup.

Unknown to anyone else—besides Teresa who had become her closest confidant—Nina attempted to woo her husband with his old Sicilian folk magic.

Did it change Nick? No, not at all.

He remained as nasty and cold as ever toward his wife. But desperate people do desperate things, and there was no question that poor Nina was desperate.

Chapter Thirty-One

Almost a year after leaving Sicily, Nina received word from her parents.

It was a cold Sunday afternoon, near the end of February. Snow piled on the ground outside. Lilly and Gina loved it. The two played outside. Nina huddled close to the radiator while she watched them through the window.

The phone rang.

Nina answered, and at the sound of her mother's voice, her face grew beet red from excitement.

"How are you? How are the children?"

"Good Mamma!" Nina exclaimed. "We have our own apartment. The kids are making a snowman outside. How are you? How is my baby girl, Diana?"

Silence came from the other end.

"Mamma?"

There was a sob. Her mother was crying.

Panic rose in Nina. "What's wrong? Is Diana okay? Please, Mamma, talk to me. I'm dying here. Is she alright?"

"Yes. Yes, she's okay. But I need to tell you something." There was another long pause. "Last night, Diana eloped with an older man."

For a moment, time seemed to stop. Nina heard her heart pounding in her chest, yet the rest of her remained frozen. Diana had only just turned eighteen. She was still a baby in her mother's eyes.

Nina dropped to her knees. Tears, loud and uncontrollable poured from her eyes. It was like someone had switched on a fountain.

"Mamma what are you saying? She can't. She can't!"

Her mother remained mute.

Through her tears, Nina continued, "Why? Why God? How much more can I take? I can't take any more, Mamma. I can't. She's a baby. Who is this bastard?"

"A teacher from Bagheria."

"Was he her teacher?" Nina could already guess the answer. "Oh God! No. Where is she now?"

"This all happened last night, sometime around nine o'clock."

That didn't answer Nina's question. "Where is she, Mamma? Do you know?"

"She's not hurt. She called last night because she didn't want me to worry."

"Why aren't you telling me where she is?"

"Because she wouldn't tell me, Nina. All Diana said was that she'd call me in a few days, and then she hung up."

"But why would she do that?"

Voice soft and sad, Nina's mother said, "I don't know, *sangu mio*."

"Could she have been taken by force?"

"Maybe. The *maresciallo* said it was a possibility."

Nina clutched her chest, gasping for air. "Oh my God. It gets worse by the minute. Why would the marshall think that?"

"He only said it's a possibility," Nina's mother said. She didn't want to worry her daughter more.

"Mamma, when she calls back, you need to tell her that her mother is dying with worry. Tell her to call me as soon as possible. But, let her know I'm not mad at her," Nina added, managing to squeeze back her tears for a moment. "I just need to hear her voice. Please, let her know."

The two said their goodbyes and hung up their phones.

Now alone in the room, without even her mother's voice, Nina's tears came again.

I set this pattern for her by eloping with Nick, she thought. *This is my fault more than hers.*

Nina hugged her feet to her chest, curling into a ball and sobbing. She didn't even notice when her daughters came in from the snow.

"Mamma, what's the matter? Why are you crying?" Lilly asked. "Did Papa hurt you?"

"No, *sangu mio*," Nina assured the little girls, looking at her with wide, worried eyes. "I burned my toe on the radiator."

"You'll be okay, Mamma," Gina assured her.

Lilly wanted to make her mother's boo-boo better. Uncertain which toe had been injured, she kissed them all.

Shaking, Nina pulled her daughters into a tight hug. She loved them, but she couldn't confide the truth in her children.

Across the street, the lights turned on in Teresa's house.

***

Nina bundled up her kids in clean dry clothes, dressed them back in their coats, and then ran with them across the street.

She rung her neighbor's doorbell and announced herself through the intercom. "Teresa, it's me Nina."

"Nina?" Her neighbor's voice came back. "*Che ce?*"

The gate opened. Teresa appeared at the door, motioning for them to hurry inside and escape the cold.

At once, Nina started to cry. She sent the girls to play in the living area and began telling her friend about the phone call she'd just received.

Lilly and Gina peeped over the couch into the kitchen. They saw the tears rolling down their mother's face.

"Is Mamma telling you about her burned toe?" Gina asked Teresa.

"Tell her yes," Nina whispered.

As instructed, Teresa turned to the little girl and said, "Yes, your silly goose mamma burned her toe."

Gina burst into laughter. "Mamma, she just called you silly goose!"

Nina just managed to smile behind her tears.

Teresa sat her down, trying to calm her. "Don't worry about Diana. She's probably being secretive because he was her teacher, and he needs to hide his ass to avoid problems with the law. You know how it is in Sicily. Once your mother goes to the priest and explains that no one was forced and that they love each other, the priest will get the *marasciallo* to overlook everything. Trust me, Nina. Diana will call you soon and tell you everything worked out for the best. Come, let me make you some tea."

Nina wiped her face, managing a vague smile. "Maybe I should give some to my kids too."

"Yes, I'll make for all of you—nice hot cups of apple cinnamon chamomile. It works magic when I'm upset or tired. Soothes you so you'll sleep like a baby."

They drank their tea, and Nina calmed down.

"*Grazie, mia cara amica,*" she said to her neighbor before leaving.

Teresa smiled. She too thought of Nina as a dear friend. "Goodnight. I hope all of you sleep well."

And with that, Nina and her daughters trekked back to their house, a little calmer than before.

Chapter Thirty-Two

Throughout Nina's months at the apartment, Signora Anna called often. The old woman liked to check in and ensure all was well.

One day, however, she called with a different purpose.

Nina took the call in her kitchen, leaning against the counter with the phone pressed to her ear. Signora Anna started the conversation the way she always did, inquiring after Nina and the girls.

Then she asked, "So how is Nicola?"

"Good. He's changed so much," Nina said. It was the same lie she always told. As much as she loved Signora Anna, Nina worried that if the older woman learned the truth, she'd call her brother and tell him everything. There was no telling what Carlo would do then.

"I'm happy for you, *figlia mia*. You went through enough," Signora Anna said. Then she shifted to the real reason she'd called. "Listen, Nina, I've got some news you may like. My nephew just graduated from university and they're throwing him a big party. Naturally, as his aunt, I'm invited, and I'd like you to be my plus-one."

"Oh, Signora Anna, *ma quanto ti voglio bene?*" Nina said, expressing her love for the older woman. "I'm so sorry, but please, try to understand me. I would love to go! But I can't. How could I? I don't have the money for a gift. I don't have a party dress. And what would I do with my kids? If they come, I'll need to buy clothes for them too. I'm honored you asked, but it's just not possible."

"The key words were when you said *I would love to go*," Signora Anna informed her. "*Ascoltami,* when we hang up, call Signora Teresa and ask her to watch your kids tomorrow morning. I'll come and pick you up with my driver, and we'll go buy you a beautiful outfit. Don't' worry about a gift. You're my guest. *Hai capito?*"

Nina understood, but still felt this was too much. "Oh no, Signora Anna, after everything you've done for me, how could I accept?"

"You're doing me the favor. I don't want to go alone. I don't know my nephew's friends. To be honest with you, I don't even know what field he's going into."

Nina giggled, tapping the phone cord with her finger. "How do you always convince me?"

Signora Anna grinned on the other end. "Be ready by nine, and don't forget to call Teresa."

* * *

The following morning, Signora Anna and Nina went shopping.

Their first stop was a high-end bridal boutique on fifth avenue. In addition to wedding gowns, they sold couture evening dresses.

Nina almost fainted when she saw the price tags.

"*Lascia stare,*" Signora Anna said, waving her hand in dismissal of any future objections. "I told you, I got this."

Nina selected a black cocktail dress. She loved it the moment she saw it on her. It fit her like a glove while the cut remained classy and conservative.

"If it's for an afternoon event, you can style it with any color," the saleswoman advised.

"Or I could wear it to a funeral," Nina joked. To herself, she added, *But not my husband's. I'll wear red when he dies.*

* * *

The party was scheduled for the next weekend at the exclusive Amalfi Lemon Orchards.

Nina avoided calling Signora Anna too much prior to the event. It seemed that every time they talked, the old woman took it upon herself to buy something else. Already, she'd gifted Nina with the dress, a designer bag, and a pair of netting gloves with ruffled cuffs. She'd booked appointments for professional hair and makeup.

When the day arrived, Nina looked like she belonged on the cover of *Vogue*.

She gathered her new clutch purse and smoothed the black dress. The hair and make-up artist had left her house a few minutes prior. Nina was ready to go.

She grabbed her keys and went to the door. It swung open before she reached it.

Who should enter but the devil himself.

Nick stared her up and down. "What did you do? Hit the Lotto?"

Without responding, Nina stepped past him, walked out and slammed the door.

He remained in the kitchen alone, mouth open like a pig.

* * *

It was a twenty-minute drive to The Amalfi Lemon Orchards in Westbury, Long Island.

Nina's hands started to sweat. She didn't know if it was nerves or the gloves.

The entrance to the reception area had been decorated with lemons and vines. Nina entered with Signora Anna. They were immediately greeted by waiters with tall glasses of champagne.

Signora Anna studied the guests in attendance. There were a few relatives she recognized, but most were strangers. She spotted a lot of men dressed in sharp dark suits. They must have been her nephew's colleagues. He'd had a job while attending graduate school, though Signora Anna still hadn't learned what field he was in.

The guests were shown to their seats. Signora Anna and Nina found themselves with six dark-suited gentlemen at their table.

"Anna, so good to see you!" Her cousin, the graduate's mother approached when they were on their second glasses of champagne. She hugged Signora Anna, who introduced Nina.

"Good to meet you dear," the cousin said. "Have you made the acquaintance of the others at your table?"

Signora Anna shook her head.

The cousin went around, giving each of their names. Then, she said, "Better known as New York's finest INS agents."

Had a surgeon performed an autopsy on Signora Anna, not a drop of blood would've been found in her system. INS stood for Immigration and Naturalization.

What have I brought this poor child into?

Nina didn't understand a word of the exchange. They'd been speaking in English, and even after all this time in America, she still struggled with the language.

Signora Anna looked and felt like the walking dead. She caught Nina's eye and twitched her head in motion that said *let's get out of here.*

Nina, all smiles and giggles, missed the fear in Signora Anna's eyes. It took a few more tries before she even noticed something was wrong.

"Do you need to use the bathroom?" Nina asked.

"Yes."

"Aww is that it? Why didn't you say so?" Nina stood and bowed politely to the gentlemen. "*Scusami.*"

The two women walked to the bathroom. Once they were inside, Signora Anna pulled Nina into the stall with her.

"*Ma che succeed, Signora Anna?*" Nina had no idea what was happening so needed to ask.

Signora Anna responded with a whisper so soft, even Nina barely heard. "Those men at our table are immigration agents. My nephew works with them."

"*Ma che cazzo mi dice, Anna?*" Nina's freight made her forget her manners. She'd dropped the *Signora* and used harsh language. "How do we get out of here?"

"I'll tell my cousin you think you have a virus. They get scared the minute someone says virus. Just stay in here and don't move. I'll be right back."

Nina remained hidden in the stall, heart pounding so loud it drummed inside her ears, waiting for the older woman to return.

* * *

There was chaos outside when Signora Anna stepped out. She turned to the man closest to her. "What's going on?"

"Someone tipped them off that there's a fugitive here," he explained. "The department doesn't take it lightly when a person escapes from under their nose. They just made an announcement. Everyone is to remain here."

Three words repeated in panic within Signora Anna's mind: Oh. My. God.

Oh my God, oh my God, oh my God.

Signora Anna stepped away slowly. She needed to get back to poor Nina, still hiding in the bathroom.

One of the agents spotted her moving. "Ma'am. You need to stay in your seat."

Anna continued backing away, pretending not to have heard.

"Ma'am, you can't move," he said more forcefully.

"I need to use the bathroom. Should I raise my hand like in kindergarten?" Signora Anna's voice rose, annoyance masking her fear.

Her cousin overheard and approached. "Are you serious?" she asked the agent. "Do you know who you're talking to? This is my cousin. She's the sister of Carlos Esteban. Are you familiar with that name?"

Recognition flashed in the agent's eyes.

The cousin continued anyway. "He's donated hundreds of thousands of dollars to your agency, and he's a close personal friend with your Security Chief Director and Deputy Director Higgins in Washington. If his sister needs to use the ladies' room, you'd better let her."

"Apologies, ma'am," the agent said.

Signora Anna accepted and hurried to the bathroom.

Nina was still hiding in the stall.

"It's me, Anna. Come out, we're leaving now."

Nina opened the door. Signora Anna grabbed her hand. They needed to get out the building.

Another INS agent waited by the elevator.

Signora Anna spotted him before he saw them. She pulled Nina back and turned them to the stairs instead. They hurried down.

They were on the last step when an agent stepped in front of them. "Ma'am where are you going? You need authorization—"

"Must we go through all this again," Signora Anna snapped, puffing herself up. "Call your director upstairs and inform him that Ms. Esteban would like to go home with her sick daughter. Is that okay?"

There was such an air of authority to the old woman that the agent complied. His director—recognizing the name at once—approved the request. A few minutes later, the agent was apologizing to them. He even held the door open so they could leave.

Signora Anna's driver waited for them outside.

Nina's mouth dropped in disbelief the moment she was safely in the car. Her heart had never beat so fast. "Signora Anna, I cannot believe the way you handled that."

"Listen my sweet girl, when you're in a situation that seems impossible or dangerous, the first thing you must do is stay calm. If you get flustered, it shows your weakness, and they'll know you're hiding something. If you're confident, they'll assume the opposite. Let that be a lesson to you, *car amia*." Then, Signora Anna chuckled. "We almost had dinner with the wolves."

Nina didn't have it in her to laugh.

"Come, let's get you home and pick up the kids. I'm dying to see them." Signora Anna patted Nina's knee.

The car headed toward Dyker Heights. As she approached her home, Nina settled down enough to think.

"How did they know to look for me?" she asked.

"I don't know. Someone said they got a tip that there was an escaped fugitive at the celebration."

"Oh my God."

They were both quiet for a moment.

Nina's thoughts continued to spin. "Just as I was leaving, Nick spotted me. You don't think..."

"That bastard!" Signora Anna slammed her hand on the seat. Although Nina had been cautious with what she'd shared, the older woman had never believed that Nick had changed his ways. "It must've been him that tipped them off. Who else could have known? When he saw you all dressed up, he must have guessed where you were going and made the call. Either him or his *buttana*. What a slimy, despicable human being to rat out his own wife!"

Nina nodded. "I think this is another lesson. Trust no one. But I must stay calm, isn't that right Signora Anna?"

"Brava, Nina! You're learning."

"Yes, though I'd prefer not to have so many lessons."

* * *

When they went to pick up the children, Teresa was concerned why they'd returned so early from the party.

"I'll tell you tomorrow," Nina said. "Right now, I need to get inside and take this dress of and wash my face."

"But you look so beautiful! Don't let anyone take that away from you." Teresa always had the nicest words for her, and Nina felt them.

"*Ma chi si duci, Tere,*" Nina said, letting her friend know how sweet she was.

Signora Anna stayed played with the children for a while before departing. Soon after, Nina bundled the girls up to return home as well.

Fresh snow had fallen, masking the ice with a new blanket of white. Nina had to cross carefully, trying to balance in her high heels to avoid slipping. The girls shivered beside her. They were all eager to get inside.

However, their house offered little reprieve.

"Mamma, it's more cold in here than it is outside," Gina said.

Nina wrapped her arms around herself and walked to the radiator. It was ice cold.

Meanwhile, she changed the kids into heavy pajamas and added their sweaters on top. To warm the kitchen, she turned on the oven and began making *pastina* in broth.

The sweaters and hot food helped the girls. Soon, Lilly and Gina were playing and running around.

Nina sat on the couch shivering, feeling the frost bite. No amount of broth could warm her. Her mind still spun from earlier.

Of course, it was Nicola. He called the agents on me. He must have known about the graduation party and guessed that's where I was going with Signora Anna.

Tears welled in Nina's eyes, but she didn't cry. She was too angry.

I can't believe what that bastard has turned into.

The thoughts of her own horrible husband sent Nina's mind toward her daughter in Italy. Why had Diana eloped with this older man? Did she care for him, or had she been forced? It must have been easy for her to be led astray without a parent there to guide her.

But I did the same thing, and my parents were there.

Still shivering, Nina rose to check on the daughters still under her watch. Her thoughts followed her.

Will Signora Anna tell her brother what happened today?

If she did, what would Carlo do when he found out? As much as Nina resented her husband, she couldn't wish physical pain on him. For all his cruelty, Nick was still the father of her children.

Lilly and Gina were chasing one another through the bedrooms. Their noses glowed red from the cold.

"Look Mamma," Gina called out. "I'm smoking!" She blew a puff of air. The cold made it vapor visible.

Nina smiled. "That's your breath. Come on, let's see if it's better under the blankets."

That night, she climbed into the bed with her daughters and held them close, needing to feel the warmth from their bodies.

Chapter Thirty-Three

When morning came, the house felt even colder. Nina wondered if the temperature had dropped. Teeth chattering, she walked to the window and discovered more snow. To fight the chill, the put a large pot of water to boil and warmed her hands in the steam.

The blast of a snowplow in the street woke the kids. Unlike their mother, they were delighted by the new snowfall. For them, it turned outdoors into a winter playscape where they could run and fall without fear of getting hurt.

"Mamma, look it's Teresa!" Lilly shouted from the window. "She's outside shoveling snow. Her husband is there too."

Nina joined her daughter at the window. The snow went past their neighbor's knees. There must have been over two feet.

Teresa was attempting to shovel a path. She spotted Nina and waved to her friend.

Nina opened the door and stepped out onto her patio to wave back.

"Don't leave the door open," Teresa shouted. "The heat will escape."

That would be a problem if there was any heat, Nina thought. She didn't mention that the radiators had turned off last night. Instead, she nodded and returned inside.

***

About an hour later, Teresa appeared at Nina's door holding a tray of fresh baked muffins. The minute she stepped inside, she exclaimed, "My God, Nina! It's cold in here! What happened to the heat?"

"We ate it," Nina said.

"This is nothing to joke about," Teresa said, marching to the kitchen to put down her tray. Even with gloves, her fingers felt cold. "It's twenty-eight degrees outside."

"The radiators have been off since yesterday. I thought maybe they just needed some time and then they'd come on again, but they're still off."

"Something must be wrong. Let me call Giacomo. He'll have a look."

***

Teresa's husband descended the steps to the partial basement where the furnace and the hot water boiler lived. He wasn't down long before he returned.

"The heat's been turned off deliberately. There's a lock around them that can't be opened without a key. It must have been the landlord."

"But why?" Teresa asked.

Nina was just relieved to know that it hadn't been Nick.

Teresa carried Nina and the girls across the street and called the landlord herself. The two conversed in English.

The landlord felt bad when he heard they'd spent the night in the cold. He'd assumed they would have gone elsewhere when they discovered that the heat was off. However, he'd had a clear motive for his actions.

"Mr. Niceli hasn't paid rent in three months," he informed her.

Teresa was horrified. She almost didn't want to tell Nina, but she had to know the truth.

After she hung up from the landlord, Teresa sat her at the kitchen table and explained the situation.

"You have to see it from his perspective. If he doesn't get paid rent, he doesn't have money to pay for gas or fuel. It's lucky he's continued to pay for the electricity, otherwise you'd have had no stove either."

"So it was Nick?" Nina started to cry. "When is it going to end? Every day, things get worse."

"Why don't you ask Signora Anna for help?"

"I can't. She'll tell her brother. If Signore Carlo finds out, he'll have Nick killed."

"And?" Teresa gave her a bewildered look. "Do you really care what happens to him?"

This kindness amazed Teresa. She couldn't understand how—given all the ways he'd hurt her—Nina didn't take revenge against her husband. She'd curse him, but her resentment ended there.

I've never come across such a good soul, Teresa thought. Though later that evening, when she'd share her admiration of Nina's kindness with her husband, Giacomo would offer a different perspective. *I don't call that a good soul, I call it stupid.*

"Maybe your landlord will take pity and turn the heat back on tonight, but you're staying with me today," Teresa insisted. "Go get what you'll need for yourself and the kids."

* * *

Teresa prepared a delicious dinner for all seven of them—herself, her husband and two children, and Nina and her daughters.

The four kids finished dinner, wolfed down dessert, and went to play in the basement.

"Mamma we're gonna play *ammucciareddo*," said Gina.

"It's called hide and seek," Danielle, Teresa's daughter, told her.

Nina stayed chatting in the kitchen, but her eyes were constantly on the time. When it was nearing ten thirty, she stood. "Let me go home and check. Tere, I can't thank you enough for what you've done for us."

"*Ma va*, I haven't done anything," Teresa said. "When you get across the street, if your heat is off, call me."

"*Va bene*," Nina agreed.

With wet and frozen feet, she walked across the street with her daughters. When the entered, the house remained bitter cold.

Gina puffed long breaths that rose into the air like smoke from a cigar. Lilly joined her.

Nina hurriedly changed them into their pajamas, not wanting them to be uncovered for long. She wrapped them beneath four layers of blankets. Then, to be extra careful, she threw their coats on top and climbed in with them.

* * *

Teresa awoke around three that morning.

Groggily, she rose and went to the living room. She pushed the curtains aside. The NYSD had snowplows cleaning the street.

Before returning to bed, Teresa glanced at Nina's home. The glass on the windows was fogged with condensation.

She has no heat!

Teresa rushed to the bedroom to inform her husband.

Giacomo waved away her concerns and rolled back over. "Get to bed, Teresa. They're probably snuggled beneath the blankets asleep. You told her to call if she didn't have heat. I'm sure it's fine."

"I know Nina. She has pride and she's considerate. She won't have called because she won't have wanted to bother me," Teresa explained, marching toward her closet. "I'm getting dressed and going across the street to bring them all back here."

"It's not your responsibility," Giacomo grumbled.

Teresa ignored him. Listening to her heart instead of her husband, she put on her boots and jacket and marched out into the cold.

* * *

When Teresa stepped into the house, it was just as she expected.

"Are you kidding me, Nina?" Teresa turned toward her neighbor, wrapped in a blanket before her. "I told you to call me if you didn't have heat. What were you thinking?"

"Tere, I feel horrible disturbing you and your family. I figured once we were in bed, we'd warm up."

Sobs came from the bedroom.

Nina and Teresa hurried in to find little Gina crying.

"Mamma, my toes and face feel like they're burning," she said.

The cold had dried and reddened her cheeks. She wore no socks. Through the night, Lilly must have pulled the covers off her sister, leaving Gina exposed.

Nina, who had little experience with winter, hadn't realized.

Almost in tears, Teresa hugged little Gina. "Come, *Bambolina*, let's get you to my house. I'll make you hot chocolate with whipped cream." She turned to Nina. "Get all the blankets you have. We'll bundle all of you up and get you across the street. You're staying at my house and sleeping in a warm bed."

Gina smiled. The cold had robbed her of her fire, and she didn't have the will to do more.

Lilly spoke up, however. "You're so good to us Signora Teresa. I love you."

Teresa's heart was ready to burst. *These poor kids,* she thought.

Nina bundled Lilly while Teresa took Gina. All four were in higher spirits as they tried to run across the street in all the snow, making a game of it and thinking of the warmth that waited beyond.

It was only when they got inside and removed their boots that Teresa noticed Nina's shoe. The sole had come apart from the snow. Nina had been walking on only the thin cardboard that remained inside.

"You think only Cinderella loses her shoe?" Nina joked when it was discovered.

Her laughter crushed Teresa. "*Shema*. Why didn't you say anything? That's all we need is you getting sick. Let me get you a pair of warm slippers upstairs. They might be a bit big, but at least they'll warm your feet."

* * *

Teresa had intended to prepare the pull-out couch in the living room for Nina to share with her daughters. However, a noise woke her own little girl.

Danielle came downstairs, saw Lilly and Gina and immediately insisted they sleep in her room.

"I don't think they'll do much sleeping," Nina said. "Maybe Gina will, but those two?" She pointed at Lilly and Danielle. "They'll talk and giggle all night."

"Let them giggle if they want," Teresa said. "There's no school tomorrow."

Nina hesitated. As dear a friend as her neighbor was, Nina had never spent the night in Teresa's home. It felt strange, and she would've preferred the comfort of her daughters beside her.

However, Lilly and Gina looked so excited by the prospect of an impromptu sleep over, Nina's objections died on her lips.

How can I rob them of this joy?

Nina had so little of it herself. She couldn't bear for her children to suffer with her.

Despite the hour, Teresa made chocolate chip muffins and hot chocolate with whipped cream for the kids before sending them up to bed. The women had cups of apple cinnamon tea. They retired shortly after their children.

Nina took a shower, grateful for the hot water but anxious about wasting it. She changed and climbed into the bed, cozy with extra pillows.

She had a decision to make.

Should she go back to Sicily in disgrace? Or should she continue her life in New York, hiding and living as a fugitive, with no support from her bastard of a husband?

Tears rolled down Nina's cheeks. She muffled her sobs with one of the pillows, happy that her children hadn't shared the bed with her after all.

* * *

Early the next morning, a loud ring startled Teresa into consciousness.

"Oh my God, this phone never stops," she complained, then picked it up. "Hello, who is this?"

Signora Anna responded on the other end. After an exchange of pleasantries, she asked about Nina. She was worried and wanted to speak with her.

"She's just downstairs," Teresa informed her. "I'll take the phone to her."

Nina was already dressed. She hadn't gotten much sleep with all her crying the previous night.

At learning that Signora Anna wanted to speak with her, she accepted the phone from Teresa.

"*Buon giorno, Signora Anna. Come sta?*"

"*Io sto bene.*"

Reluctant to share what had happened the previous night, Nina danced around the issue, flooding their conversation with unimportant chatter. Signora Anna waited patiently, asking just the right questions until Nina cracked, and the truth spilled from her.

"Enough is enough," Signora Anna said when she'd finished. "My brother has to know about this."

"Signora Anna, please—"

The old woman cut off her objections. "No, listen to me, Nina. You and the girls are coming to stay with me. Take what you need and bring it to my home. Don't think you have an option. I'm sending my driver to collect you at three o'clock this afternoon. You all will be my cherished guests until we resolve this situation. One way or another."

Signora Anna's tone was firm, but a dark fury trembled beneath.

Nina had never heard her speak with such anger. "Signora Anna, I have no words."

"They would be unnecessary. I know what you feel," the old woman assured her. "Now, give the phone to Teresa and go start packing. *Spicciati!*"

Nina jumped from the bed. She found Teresa in the kitchen and returned the phone to her. Despite Signora Anna's final instruction to hurry up, however, Nina lingered in the room, listening to the exchange that took place.

"Hello, Signora Anna. It's me, Teresa."

"*Ascoltami*," the old woman instructed. "What you have done for Nina and her children has earned you a favor from me. Whatever you need, whatever you wish, I am only a phone call away. I have a powerful and very wealthy brother. With his help, you can touch the clouds if that's what you want. Now, do not breathe a word to Nina of what I'm about to say next, understand?"

Teresa glanced at her neighbor, lingering in the kitchen. She pressed the phone closer to her ear.

In English, she said, "I understand."

Signora Anna caught the shift. Previously, they'd spoken Italian.

"My brother has been in communication with INS about Nina," she said, now talking English as well. She had an obvious accent, but she was fluent enough to continue. "They cannot give her asylum as my brother requested, mainly because she is a fugitive. She escaped from under the nose of the INS, and they're pretty uptight about those things. It's become a political issue at the department. Everyone knows her name. They're hunting for her and won't stop until she's apprehended. Please, don't tell her. It will only add to her problems."

Teresa felt Nina's eyes on her. She struggled to keep her expression relaxed.

"You're a good woman, Teresa. I want you to think of me as a good friend. Bless your heart!"

"*Grazie, Signora Anna,*" Teresa thanked her, returning to Italian. "I appreciate all your beautiful words, but what I'm doing for Nina, I'm doing from my heart."

Nina relaxed as she listened to the two women exchange kind words in Italian. She had no idea what they'd discussed.

Shortly after the phone conversation, Nina left, giving Teresa a fond farewell before she did.

"Tere, I have to go pack some clothes for the three of us. The driver will be here at three. I can never thank you enough, but please know, you'll always be in my heart. I've found a mother in Signora Anna and a sister in you. *Grazie. Grazie mille volte. Grazie, sangu mio.*"

Chapter Thirty-Four

Signora Anna's driver arrived on time, as usual. Nina had only one suitcase, her handbag, and carry-on with personal items and toiletries. The girls had their dolls and toys.

Despite their few belongings, Nina needed the driver to assist them. The snow made it difficult to walk and masked the icy traps beneath.

Anna's driver carried the suitcase in one arm and Gina in another. Lilly went with them, clinging to the bag's strap for support. He had to go back for Nina.

Watching from the back of the car, the girls found it amusing to see the driver holding their mother under her arm.

"If Mamma falls, she's going to pull him down," Gina said, and the two both erupted in hysterics.

* * *

Nina and the girls rode the elevator up to Signora Anna's apartment.

The older woman waited by the door. The moment Lilly and Gina stepped in, she embraced them as though they were her grandkids.

"My little cupcakes." She kissed Lilly's cheek. "My sweet little cupcakes." She kissed Gina next.

The little one cupped Signora Anna's face in her small hands. "Signora Anna, I told you. I'm no cupcake. I'm Gina."

Signora Anna smiled and kissed her nose.

Even in the midst of her problems, Nina's heart filled with warmth and love. She saw the way Signora Anna cared for them all, and she felt it too.

"Look what I made for you guys," Signora Anna said, leading them to the kitchen. "I made nice round waffles, and later, we'll put ice cream in between and we'll have ice cream sandwiches."

Gina's face lit up. "Do you have chocolate ice cream? Cause I like chocolate, and Lilly likes strawberry, and Mamma likes... uhm..." The little girl paused, brow furrowing. "Mamma, what do you like?"

Anna thought that was funny because she knew what her sister likes but did not know what her mother likes. "Oh, you sweet precious girl, you're a little firecracker."

"She really is," Nina agreed. Now that the truth had come out about Nick, she couldn't resist sharing more with Signora Anna. "Do you know that one time the *porco* took them both to his *puttana's* house. Guess what Gina did?"

Signora Anna listened to the story. By the end her face beamed with pride. She bent down wrapped Gina in her arms. "Good for you, *pupa mia*. I'd have smashed that chocolate bunny too."

Gina burst into laughter, and Nina leaned against the kitchen island. There was nothing so heartwarming and gratifying as laughter from a child.

For the first time in ages, Nina felt content.

* * *

After dinner and waffle ice cream sandwiches, the children took the elevator upstairs. Signora Anna had prepared the room she'd originally intended for them, filling it with plenty of toys.

While the two slept, Nina and Signora Anna remained on the couches. Cozy fleece blankets warmed their legs, and each sipped a hot cup of cappuccino.

Neither had any idea what was happening in the lobby.

Four federal agents had entered the building and approached George, the doorman in the lobby. They'd instructed him not to inform Ms. Anna Stefano of their presence. If George refused to comply, he'd be an accomplice, guilty of harboring a fugitive.

* * *

The elevator went straight to the top floor. From there, the only door in the foyer led to Signora Anna's penthouse.

The doorbell rang.

George didn't mention anyone coming up, Signora Anna thought.

She crossed to the door and looked through the peephole.

Three federal agents stood in the foyer beyond.

Signora Anna's heart nearly leaped from her chest. However, as she'd instructed Nina, it was crucial to remain calm.

"What's the matter?" Nina asked, approaching the door. "Who is it?"

Signora Anna put her index finger against her lips. She pulled Nina back towards the couch and whispered, "It's immigration. Sit here on the couch. Cover your legs with the blanket. I'll tell them you're my daughter and you're partially paralyzed, deaf, and mute. Nina, please, do as I say."

The old woman went back to the door. "Who is it?"

"INS agents, ma'am," the man's voice said.

Signora Anna opened the door. "Do you realize what time it is? I'm not a young chick who stays up after nine. Furthermore, you're scaring my daughter." She lowered her voice to a whisper, leaning close to the agents as though their presence didn't concern her. "Let me tell her that you all are family of ours? You see, my daughter is very ill. She's contacted a virus that's left her with some troubling side effects…"

The old woman went on to explain, and the agents' eyes turned toward the woman on the couch.

Nina sat beneath the blanket, not moving. Her face was as white as a ghost. The agents could believe she was sick.

Still keeping her voice low, as though she were afraid her daughter might overhear, Signora Anna feigned ignorance. "What brings you gentlemen to my home? Why are you here?"

"It is Ms. Stefano, is it not?" one of the agents asked.

"It most certainly is. After my husband passed twenty-two years ago, I took back my birth name."

"Ms. Stefano, we were instructed to come to your residence in search of a Mrs. Nina Niceli. She's a fugitive from our department. Are you familiar with her?"

"Of course, I know her. She was here just an hour ago. I have no idea where she went when she left, but she's certainly not here. You're welcome to search the apartment if you wish, but please try to be quiet. My grandkids are sleeping upstairs."

One of the agents searched, obliging Signora Anna's request. The other two remained in the room.

One sat on the club chair. The other took the love seat across from Nina.

"How do you know Mrs. Niceli, ma'am?" one of them asked.

Cool as a bird, Signora Anna answered honestly. "We met on a cruise and became friends when we discovered we came from nearby towns. We arrived in Miami together, but parted ways after that."

"But she came to visit you today?"

"Yes, I'd given her my phone number and address back on the ship. I didn't think she intended to reach out and was quite surprised when she showed up today. She seemed nervous. I think she's planning to go back to Sicily. I assume she had an issue with her husband. He lives here in the city. But I'm only guessing. I know very little about her."

"There's no one here, just the kids sleeping in their room," the third agent announced, returning from his search. However, he held something in his hand—Nina's suitcase.

The agent lifted it onto the top of the couch, undid the claps, and opened the lid.

"And these Ms. Stefano? Whose articles of clothing are they? They surely don't look like they could fit you."

Signora Anna stared at him with a look of great offense. "I beg your pardon, sir. How dare you go through my daughter's belongings? Should I also have told you that she's staying with me because she's presently having marital problems at home? Well, I do apologize. I assumed that my personal life and my daughter's own had nothing to do with this search of yours. Is there any more sensitive information you'd like to pry into?"

"It's just—" the agent tried to say, but she interrupted him.

"I told you the truth about Mrs. Niceli. But now you're invading my family's privacy, Mister… I'm sorry, I didn't get your name? I'd love to write a letter of recommendation on your behalf. You were so observant, noticing that my daughter's clothing couldn't fit me, and so tactful to point it out. Really, my compliments, sir."

The startled agent closed the suitcase. He knew—as did they all—who Signora Anna's brother was.

"Ms. Stefano, please accept our deepest apology," the agent seated on the club chair said. "We're all human beings and sometimes we make mistakes. Thank you for your time and honesty."

The agents stood, and Signora Anna led them back to the foyer.

Nina had escaped INS for the third time.

Chapter Thirty-Five

With the agents gone, the color returned to Nina's face. Her virus was cured. She sighed in relief and leaned back against the couch.

Signora Anna joined her.

Nina was amazed by the older woman's performance. She couldn't believe how Signora Anna had handled the agents.

"I've never seen anyone perform so well under such pressure," Nina said. "You were more in control than the agents. I think your confidence left the one interrogating you dumbfounded."

The phone rang beside Signora Anna. Still shaken from what had just happened, she answered quickly, anxious as to who might be on the other end.

It was Teresa.

Signora Anna relaxed. "*Ciao, mia cara Teresa.* Let's just say, things could be better."

"*Perche che ce?*" Teresa asked.

"We had visitors from INS," Signora Anna explained.

Teresa gasped.

Before she could say anything, Signora Anna continued. "Listen to me, my sweet Teresa, try to understand every word I tell you because the walls, the phone, the plants all have ears, and my grandchildren are sleeping. They were sleeping when the agents searched upstairs, you follow?"

"Yes, Signora."

"These visitors interrogated me about Mrs. Nina Niceli. I don't know if you know her. I was at home with my handicapped daughter, who is seated on the couch with me now. I told the agents that Mrs. Niceli had visited me earlier, but had left, possibly to return to Sicily."

"I see. But you and your daughter and grandkids are fine?"

"Yes, there's no need to worry about us."

"I'm glad," Teresa said. She paused, trying to think how to explain why she'd called. "I wanted to mention to you that as soon as that young mother left today, her husband came here looking for her. I told him truthfully where she was. I'm so sorry. He told me he wanted to take care of her. I think the bastard may have been looking to hurt her instead."

"My daughter and I are coming into Brooklyn tomorrow to do some shopping," Signora Anna said. "Let's meet and have lunch."

"Yes, that sounds like a great idea. I'm dying to see your daughter again."

* * *

Nina listened as Signora Anna explained what Nick had done. She'd already been struggling to absorb what had happened with the federal agents. Learning that her husband had sent them to her again was too much.

"I feel like a walking dead person," she said.

Nina curled her legs beneath the blanket, unable to believe what was happening.

That bastard! Someone ought to spit in his face.

"Signora Anna, if I go back to Sicily, it's because I don't want to put you in danger with the law. You have done a world of good for me, and I will never forget your kindness. Now, however, it's my turn to think of you. Can we pass by the house tomorrow? I need to get the rest of my stuff."

"No problem, Nina, I'll have the driver take us there after lunch with Teresa."

* * *

The following morning started off like a dream.

Signora Anna took Nina shopping at the Italian Market. The smell of fresh roasted coffee rose from the café bar. Shops displayed balls of fresh mozzarella, bottles of cured olives, and long coils of fennel sausage. Stalls sold Signora Anna's favorite *babbaluci,* a Sicilian delicacy of small snails.

People crowded the market, calling to one another and purchasing items. Nina understood the snippets of conversation she overheard.

They're speaking in Italian.

She headed down to 18th Avenue, where the aroma of the hot semolina bread floated out of the ovens of one of the bakeries. The scent nearly pulled her inside. The owners were from Palermo, and the pastries, the cookies, the cassatas, the gelato all tasted the same as her hometown sweets in Sicily. Nearby were others selling fresh pasta and raviolis.

It was all a sweet memory of home.

Their lunch with Teresa continued the trend. Signora Anna took them all—Nina, Teresa, and their daughters—to a restaurant on 4th Avenue that she'd been hoping to try. The owners were Italians, who oversaw all the cooking.

"Wow," Nina said, as she stepped through the door. She stared at the packed round tables. "I think there's more Italians here than in Bagheria."

The comment earned her a laugh from both Signora Anna and Teresa.

After a few minutes wait, a waitress took the party of six to one of the tables.

With the girls distracted with their own conversation, Teresa leaned over and whispered to Nina, "I understood all that Signora Anna said to me last night. I'm hurting so much for you, but he hasn't won yet

—*Bastardo di cane!* You have Signora Anna and me in your corner, and we'll always be there for you."

Her friend's kind words meant the world to Nina. She almost cried.

The group of six ordered lunch. Pizza and fries for the girls. Teresa enjoyed the pasta seafood marinara, while both Signora Anna and Nina had the salsa *arrabiata* seafood over linguine.

"We're so Italian," Teresa joked when the plates arrived. "Look at us, we all ordered pasta."

They, they talked, they laughed. The girls had dessert—gelato for Lilly and Daniela, tiramisu for little Gina. The adults shared some wine.

For Nina, it was a perfect meal. In those moments, she forgot all about the federal agents.

However, they hadn't forgotten about her.

Chapter Thirty-Six

Dyker Heights was only a short drive away. Most of the snow had melted and the streets were cleared.

Teresa and Danielle got a lift with Signora Anna's driver. Nina intended to go home to gather more of her belongings.

When they arrived, however, Teresa invited them all to come into her home. Her son and husband were at a soccer game.

"Stay for dinner," Teresa suggested. Although they'd just eaten, Nina and Signora Anna happily agreed. Both were enjoying the company and neither wanted the day to end.

A delighted Lilly and Gina raced with Danielle up to her room, leaving the adults to chat in the kitchen. They'd kept their conversation light and cheerful over lunch. Now, in the privacy of Teresa's home, they were able to discuss the incident with the federal agents and Nina's situation in more detail.

Their conversation stretched hours, and soon Teresa was summoning the girls to the kitchen to help her with dinner.

"Don't make anything too complicated," Nina said. "I know you love to cook, but we just had pasta. A *secondi* and a light salad *e basta*."

"Ouuu, this *mia casa*," Teresa said with a grin. "*Tu casa*, you're the boss."

Nina hugged her friend. "*Sì, cara.* You're the boss of your house, but I'm the boss of my stomach."

They all laughed.

"Teresa, do you need help?" Signora Anna asked.

"No, I have my three little helpers right." Teresa grinned and pointed at the three girls who'd arrived in the kitchen. "Tonight, I teach them how to cook Sicilian style."

"Come then, Nina," Signora Anna said. "Let's get your stuff from the house."

* * *

The last hints of daylight still lingered in the sky, but a chill nipped at the air.

Nina crossed the street, a few paces ahead of her friend. She reached into her pocket, focused on getting her keys out so she could open the door.

Signora Anna stopped near the edge of Teresa's property. A car, pulled over to the side, had caught her eye. It sat on the road as though it was waiting for someone. The old woman squinted, trying to see through the window.

Inside was a familiar face—Nick Niceli.

He was in the car with two other men. Signora Anna recognized one of them as well. He'd been at her house the night before.

In that moment, the old woman's voice failed her. Only her mind screamed out: *Immigration is here!*

Ahead of Signora Anna, Nina remained oblivious.

She found her keys in the pocket and unlocked the door. Feet sounded on the lawn behind her. Nina didn't turn. She assumed it was Signora Anna—

Until an immigration agent grabbed her upper arm.

* * *

Nina twisted, trying to get the man away from her. She had no idea what was happening. She turned and her eyes moved from her home to the street. A second federal agent was climbing her stairs while a third blocked the middle of the street, attempting to stop Signora Anna from reaching her.

Behind them all, standing at the side of the road by an unfamiliar car, was Nick.

Just then, everything clicked for Nina.

"You bastard!" She screamed at him from the top of her lungs. "You bastard!"

Despite the agent holding her upper arm, Nina flung herself down the stairs. She escaped his grasp and the scrambling hands of his partner long enough to rush toward her husband.

Nick was too startled to move.

When Nina got close enough, she spat twice in his face.

"I promised myself I would do that before I left!" she shrieked. "You deserve it!"

* * *

Inside her house, Teresa heard the scream. She rested down her chef's knife and ran outside. The girls, who'd been helping her in the kitchen ran upstairs to get a better view from the front window.

Two little faces pressed against the glass. Little Gina was too short to reach. This might have been a blessing.

Lilly saw everything.

Her mother being slapped with handcuffs. Her father watching coldly from the side. Her mother passing out, falling toward the ground. A federal agent catching her.

Desperate tears streamed down Lilly's face.

The ever-determined Gina grabbed a chair and pulled it toward the window. She climbed on top in time to see her mother being carried away.

"Mamma!" Gina banged both fists on the window. Soon, she was crying as well, sobbing alongside her sister.

* * *

The agents carried Nina into her house. Teresa went with them.

Signora Anna did not.

The old woman slipped away.

Her driver waited nearby. Signora Anna climbed into the car. She didn't go anywhere. Instead, she lifted the phone and called her brother.

When Carlo answered, Anna told him everything: how Nick had been treating Nina, how he'd stopped paying rent, how he'd called the INS multiple times.

On the other end, Carlo's fist clenched tighter with every word. He'd had no idea.

"I'll handle this," Carlo said to his sister. "First with Immigration, then with Niceli. Go inside and help Nina. She must have come to by now. Where are the kids?"

Anna's eyes squeezed shut. "They saw everything. I spotted them in tears at the window."

"Bastard. That son of a bitch, despicable bastard," Carlo spat the insults out, shaking with fury. "He'll pay for this. He'll pay big time."

* * *

"Lilly! Gina!" Signora Anna called to the girls as she went into Teresa's house.

The moment they heard her voice, they rushed down the stairs. Their faces were wet and red from their tears.

Signora Anna wrapped them in her arms, pulling them close to her heart. She caressed their faces and kissed the tops of their heads. "It's okay, baby. Everything is going to be all right. No more crying. Mamma is across the street. She's not hurt. She's going to be fine. Come, wash your faces, and we can go see her."

The poor kids were so eager to get to their mamma they forgot to put on socks.

* * *

Across the street, Nina sat on her cold couch. She'd fainted for only a brief spell and had come to in the agent's arms. Teresa sat beside her, translating the questions of the two men with them.

The agent in charge had stepped outside. A message had come through on his pager, and much like Signora Anna, he'd gone to the car to make a call of his own.

Lilly and Gina burst through the door. Signora Anna followed behind them.

The girls rushed to their mother, wrapping their arms around her.

Nina kissed their heads. She couldn't hug them back. Suddenly, the thought of being taken away and leaving all three of her daughters without their mother became too much. Nina burst into tears. Soon, she and the two girls were all inconsolable.

The agent in charge stepped inside. It was the same man who'd visited Signora Anna's apartment the previous night. He wore a deep scowl on his face as he glared at the old woman.

"My superior's just informed me that Mrs. Niceli won't be coming back with us. Instead, she's been allowed to stay at home, providing she wears an ankle monitor. A fortuitous turn of events for her since illegal immigrants who enter without proper authorization can be imprisoned for up to two years."

Nina remained sobbing until Teresa translated what he was saying.

"Wealth and power shouldn't place anyone above the law," the agent continued, glaring at Signora Anna. "Yet you vanished to your car and now our orders have suddenly changed. I wonder who you called."

It wasn't a question. The agent had no doubt.

Signora Anna bristled at the agent's tone. "Excuse me, sir—no one here is trying to be above the law. You have your orders, and we are following them. I don't know what you're trying to insinuate, but I hope you have proof before you start making accusations. Especially considering your new orders come from one of your superiors."

The other two agents lifted their brows, giving the one in charge concerned glances. It didn't look good to question the chain of command.

"Of course, you're right, Ms. Stefano." The lead agent's lips twisted in an unpleasant smile. "Our new order is to keep Mrs. Niceli under house arrest until she departs for Sicily. You did say that's what your friend was planning—or, sorry, is it your daughter?"

Signora Anna kept her expression cool, but her stomach turned. Lying to a federal agent was a crime. She'd hoped the agent wouldn't recognize Nina from the previous night, but his comment made it clear that he had.

One of the other men fetched the ankle monitor and placed it on Nina's ankle. He was gentler that the lead agent.

"Is this your residence here in the U.S.?" he inquired.

Nina and her daughters had stopped crying. The two girls sat on one side of their mother. Teresa sat on the other. She would have translated, but Signora Anna answered the questions on Nina's behalf.

"This has been her residence," the old woman said. "But today it was brought to my attention that the heating system is not working. As you can see, it is unlivable. If the agency permits, Mrs. Niceli can stay in my residential home with me, and I'll post any bond that the law requires to keep her free."

"I think someone's already dealt with the money," the lead agent muttered. However, he went to speak with his superior officer once again. It was a shorter discussion this time, and he returned quickly to say that Signora Anna's request had been approved.

Nina almost started crying again from relief when her friends explained.

The agents had Signora Anna sign certain documents in the cold kitchen. Meanwhile, Nina and the girls packed the remainder of their things, assisted by their loving neighbor.

"Tomorrow morning, I'm coming to see you in the apartment," Teresa informed the girls as they gathered the last of their clothes. "So have hot chocolate ready for me, and don't forget the whipped cream."

Lilly and Gina smiled, though their hearts didn't feel it.

Chapter Thirty-Seven

Previously, Signora Anna's home had been a security blanket for Nina. Simply being within had given her a sense of safety.

Not tonight.

Nina's security blanket had been stripped away. Sitting on the couch with a strange device locked to her ankle, she felt alone, desperate, and scared.

The room was silent. Nina clutched her daughters' hands, one on each side. All three stared at the room with vacant eyes. Tears streamed down Nina's face, but she didn't sob or make a noise. Occasionally, Gina reached up to wipe her mother's tears.

Signora Anna joined them with a sympathetic smile. Her heart broke for them all. She tried to make conversation.

Nina was too weak to respond.

"Mamma's tired," Lilly defended her mother's silence. "Maybe that's why she doesn't answer."

Signora Anna's eyes watered. "I know sweetheart. She's probably so tired because of all the shopping we did today."

The old woman wished she knew the right words. She wanted to comfort the children, but she worried anything else she said might make her cry too.

Someone has to be strong for these precious, innocent children, Signora

Anna thought. She made an excuse to go downstairs so she could let out her tears.

"Don't move from the couch," she told the girls. "Stay here with Mamma."

It was only after her friend left that Nina finally managed a whisper, so soft her daughters missed it.

"I'm dying. That man's been killing me slowly since the day we met."

* * *

Signora Anna stepped outside to get a breath of fresh air. Two unmarked black cars waited outside the building. She recognized one of the federal agents who'd accompanied them from Dyker Heights leaning against one. Another patrolled the sidewalk, circling the building.

Wolves waiting for a lamb to slaughter, Signora Anna thought.

The old woman shivered, turned, and retreated inside.

George, who'd been apologetic since allowing the agents in the night before, hurried to help her to the elevator. He was quick to inquire if everything was okay as they ascended.

"Yes, of course. Don't worry." Signora Anna reassured the doorman with a smile. The truth would have been more complicated, and she didn't want George feeling guilty. Nothing that had happened with the agents was his fault. He'd only done his job allowing them up to the penthouse.

Signora Anna let herself into the apartment.

Lilly remained next to her mamma as she'd been instructed. Gina had climbed onto Nina's lap. The little girl tidied her mother, combing one hand through her hair while applying lipstick with the other.

This act finally stirred Nina from her silence. She wrapped her hands around Gina's shoulders and pulled her face toward her heart.

"Mamma, I can't breathe," Gina objected.

If she'd had the strength, Nina would have laughed. But all she could muster was a small smile. "I'm sorry, *pupa mia*."

Nina released Gina and leaned to kiss Lilly's head.

Signora Anna watched for a moment before stepping into the space and reclaiming her seat. "Is there any love for me?"

Lilly stood and went to the old woman. "I love you a lot, Signora Anna."

"I love you too, my sweet Lilly." Signora Anna embraced the girl. "Now guys, my stomach is asking *why is there no food coming down?*"

Gina laughed. "You're silly, Signora Anna. Your stomach can't talk."

The comment got Nina's attention as well. With eyes still half vacant, she turned to the old woman. "Thank you, Signora Anna, but I'm really not hungry."

"Understandable, but come and sit at the table with the kids. Maybe you'll manage a few bites."

* * *

The next morning, Nina and Signora Anna had a surprise visitor.

George rang from downstairs to inform them. "There's a lady here name Teresa who would like to come up."

"Yes, let her in," Signora Anna said. "She's a dear friend of ours."

She went to tell Nina, who sat on the couch staring at her daughters. Lilly and Gina had no idea that the device on their mother's ankle confined her to the apartment. The two girls, still in their pajamas, were having a wonderful morning playing with their dolls. When they heard Teresa was on her way up, however, both kids abandoned their toys and rushed to the door.

Happy to see her friend but burdened by the stress of her situation, Nina followed more slowly.

Signora Anna opened the door, and Teresa stepped in.

"Where's Daniela?" Gina demanded at once, staring into the hall toward the elevator.

"She had to go to school today," Teresa explained.

Gina made a face. Evidently, she did not approve.

Signora Anna chuckled and sent the two girls upstairs. Gina continued to look bothered by their friend's absence. Lilly, however, gave the adults a polite goodbye.

Once they were alone, Teresa turned to Nina. "What's going on? Did you decide what you're doing?"

"Signora Anna has spoken with her lawyer," Nina said, walking Teresa toward the kitchen. "He's going to get in touch with an immigration lawyer and have them give us a call."

"One day before you leave, or even if you stay, I want you to come over for dinner," Teresa said. The meal she'd planned for the previous night had been interrupted. "And Signora Anna, I'm sure this goes without saying, but you are invited as well. I think of you as Nina's family and a dear friend of mine."

"*Grazie, Teresa*. We think of you as Nina's sister."

Teresa hugged them both before she left.

* * *

Nina had no choice but to spend the day in the penthouse. Her daughters, however, got a treat. Signora Anna took them shopping at an American Doll store near Rockefeller Plaza.

Lilly and Gina stepped inside, and their mouths opened in awe. They'd never seen such beautiful dolls with so many outfits.

One of the dolls was named Bianca. Lilly lifted her up at once. "This was my make-believe name while we were on the cruise. Do you remember, Signora Anna?"

"I certainly do." The old woman had thought the girls were named Bianca and Aurora for the first few weeks they'd known one another. "Should we take her home with us?"

Lilly was thrilled. By the time they left the store, she had both the Bianca doll and another with dark curly hair, just like hers. Gina likewise had a doll that resembled her and a second one wearing a felt beret and glasses. Both girls had purchased accessories and outfits, for their toys and themselves.

"We can all wear matching pajamas," Lilly said in excitement, staring into the bag at the nightgown she'd bought to match with her dolls.

Signora Anna beamed as she saw the joy on the girls' faces. She loved the children as though they were her own grandchildren and would've purchased even more gifts for them were it not for their mother's situation. If Nina had to travel back to Sicily, the airplane's weight restrictions would limit how much they could carry.

"Signora Anna," Gina said, tugging at the older woman's sleeve as they went to leave the store. "We have to buy something for Mamma."

Forget weight limits for now, Signora Anna thought. "You're absolutely right."

* * *

"Oh my goodness!" Nina exclaimed as they burst through the door. "Did you guys buy the entire store?"

"Mamma, Mamma!" Gina rushed to her on the loveseat. "The dolls have pajamas, and me and Lilly got the same pajamas as our dolls. I love Signora Anna!"

"There's something for you too, Mamma," Lilly said.

"For me?" Nina wasn't sure if they were serious. "No, I'm too old for dolls."

"It's not a doll," Signora Anna said. She pulled a beautifully wrapped box from one of the bags.

Surprised, Nina took the gift. She stared at it for a few moments.

Gina was too excited to wait for her mother. The little girl started tearing at the wrapping.

Within was a beautiful Gucci bag, navy with the signature red stripe logo on the side. There was a large Savoy Duffle bag to match.

"Oh Signora Anna, what am I going to do with you?" Nina ran her fingers along the expensive bags, scarcely believing they were hers. "You shouldn't have. You've already done a world of goodness for me and my children. Now this too?"

* * *

That evening, Signora Anna received a call from Henry Weaver, a defense attorney who specialized in immigration and deportation cases.

The old woman pressed the phone to her ear and leaned against the cushions. Nina sat beside her on the couch.

"Unfortunately," Henry began. "The name Nina Niceli has become known in Washington. It's become a political issue. She escaped Miami immigration agents, then evaded the ones in New York, possibly twice. However, they can't prove that she was at your home when they searched, so no charges will be pressed against you Ms. Stefano."

Signora Anna said a silent prayer. At least that was a bit of good news. "And what do you advise Mrs. Niceli to do?"

"The immigration department will want to avoid any further humiliation. If Mrs. Niceli returns to Italy, she should be able to return legally in the future. Either you or your brother can file to employ her here in the U.S. and she can get status that way. It might be a bit difficult given everything that's happened, but it should be possible, even if the process takes a while."

"What's he saying?" Nina whispered, trying to hear despite the fact that they were speaking in English.

Signora Anna held up a finger. She kept her expression calm, but she knew this news would upset Nina.

"And there's no way for her to stay?" the old woman asked.

"Mrs. Niceli didn't just overstay a visa. She broke the law when she entered. In my opinion, if she stays, she has no case."

Nina watched Signora Anna's expression for a hint of what was being said. The old woman met her eyes and shook her head.

It was a small thing. No words had been exchanged. Still, Nina understood.

Her heart stopped.

"But listen, Ms. Stefano," the lawyer continued. "I have it on good authority that the department is willing to drop the charges against her name if she leaves of her own volition."

"Yes, that's good," Signora Anna said. She thanked the lawyer before ending the call. Then, she turned to the girl beside her and translated the conversation that had occurred.

Nina stared at the wall, eyes growing more vacant with every new piece of information.

"Well, what do you think?" Signora Anna asked. "He's a very good lawyer. We should take his advice."

Nina sighed. "Then there's really only one choice."

Chapter Thirty-Eight

Signora Anna made the arrangements for the flights.
Nina packed her bags. She didn't intend to take much, only the essentials. Everything else could stay in Signora Anna's loft.
They would still be there when she returned. This was the only way to comfort herself.

Signora Anna found Nina folding her dresses in her room.

"I've purchased three plane tickets," the old woman said. "You all will leave JFK on Saturday and arrive in Rome on Sunday morning. Then you have another flight to Palermo."

Nina placed her dress in her suitcase. She couldn't think about the details of the trip right now. "Do you think I can get permission from the agents to go to dinner at Teresa's house before I leave?"

"I'll see what I can do."

* * *

Signora Anna sat on the stool in her kitchen, punching her brother's number into the phone.

When he answered, Carlo was delighted to hear her as always. However, he didn't spend long on pleasantries.

"I'm flying in Thursday night," Carlo said.

Anna paused. She was always pleased to see her brother, but this announcement worried her. "Any particular reason?"

"My godson and I have unfinished business."

Anna's chest grew tight. "Don't be too hard on him," she said, keeping her tone as light as she could manage. "He's still Lilly and Gina's father."

"They've already lost him. It would make no difference if he was dead."

A chill went through Anna. Her brother had a point, but she knew there was a reason her friend had hidden the truth of Nick's cruelty for so long. "Nina still loves him. She doesn't want you to hurt him."

Carlo was silent.

"She's flying out on Saturday."

"I know. Part of why I'm coming up." Carlo's voice grew warm and loving once more. "I want to surprise Nina and the kids before they leave. Those little girls got into my blood stream."

"I know what you mean." Anna smiled. "I had another favor to ask as well."

* * *

Nina was granted permission to leave the penthouse for an evening.

Thursday afternoon, while Nina styled herself for dinner at Teresa's house, a delivery arrived for Signora Anna. It was a wooden crate wrapped in cellophane and a big red bow. Within were four Amarone della Valpolicella Classico Riservas, a decorative box of Gran Patron Collection, with a beautiful basket of Remy Martin Louis Grande Champagne Cognac, two bottles of champagne, and a bottle of Patron XO Café Old Presentation Coffee Tequila.

"*Oh Dio mio!*" Nina exclaimed when she came downstairs and saw it by the door. "This is even greater than a wedding gift."

Signora Anna laughed. "It's to thank Teresa for all she's done for my daughter. You are my daughter, aren't you?"

"Of course, I am." Nina's smile spread across her face to hear the old woman express her love in this way. "I've never felt like anything but a daughter to you."

* * *

An unmarked car full of federal agents followed them to Teresa's house. The men watched through the windows as Nina, Signora Anna, and the girls stepped inside.

Lilly and Gina ran into Teresa's waiting arms.

"How are my two gorgeous Sicilians?" Teresa asked joyfully.

"Here we go again," Gina complained. "My name is *Gina, capisci?*"

"I'm going to bite you my beautiful Sicilian Gina."

Gina turned to her mother with a big grin. "I think she got it."

Signora Anna presented Teresa with the extravagant gift she'd brought.

"Why did you do this?" Teresa stared at all the bottles in disbelief. "I appreciate your generosity and thought, but your presence would have been more than enough for me."

"*Niente, cara mia.*" Signora Anna waved it off as though it were nothing. "Good people deserve to be acknowledged and praised. Bad people should be ignored and rejected." She looked at Nina as she offered this advice.

Teresa changed the topic. "Come, let's go to the dining room."

The table had been exquisitely laid. Teresa's best China and stemware sparkled on a light pink embroidered tablecloth. A delicious Sicilian fish salad filled a crystal bowl in the center. Beside it was a tray of assorted cubed cheeses, thin sliced prosciutto, and cracked green olives that Teresa personally made each year. Another platter displayed *caponata*, a Sicilian delicacy made with fried eggplant mixed with tomato sauce, onions, celery, and capers. Lastly, a covered oval baking dish had been filled with roasted octopus.

This alone would have been a meal sufficient for any king. However, Teresa loved to cook. She'd prepared even more.

For the first course, she brought *annelletti al forno* from her oven. The small rings of pasta were layered with chopped meat, peas, and mozzarella. For *secondi*, Teresa had prepared surf and turf—a thick wedge of filet mignon and a whole lobster oreganata for each of them. On top of that, she'd roasted lamb chops with lemon, garlic, and rosemary.

They enjoyed their food. Everyone was happy to be together again—especially the children.

Lilly had brought both of her new dolls to show Daniela. The moment they'd finished eating, they'd run to play with them in the hallway.

"Signora Anna," Lilly peeped into the dining room. "Can I ask you something?"

Amused, Signora Anna shared a look with both Nina and Teresa before going. The old woman bent down. She had no idea what the girl wanted to ask her.

Lilly whispered in her ear. "Would you be upset if I gave one of the new dolls you bought for me to Daniela?"

"Oh, my dear Lord! How much of an angel are you?" Signora Anna couldn't believe it. "Of course you can! That is the sweetest thing I've ever witnessed." She turned back to the dining room with a glow in her heart.

Other gifts were given that night as well. Teresa had purchased two gold lockets for her daughter to give to her friends. In one there was a picture of Daniella with Lilly, the other showed her with Gina.

Both girls were excited to receive the lockets—Lilly in particular.

"I'll never take this necklace off again," she said.

It was a beautiful moment, and lovely farewell. However, not everyone was in high spirits.

Despite her best efforts to remain cheerful, Nina's heart ached. What waited for them in Sicily? Would they be able to return?

Nina struggled to hide her sorrow, and her eyes betrayed her.

Lilly had learned to recognize this look in her mother. Even after she'd been dismissed to play, the girl kept coming into the dining room to check on her mother.

Teresa noticed this sadness as well. However, she had a final gift for Nina that she hoped might help.

Since learning about Nina's oldest daughter's elopement, Teresa had been in touch with her family in Bagheria. She'd learned more about Diana and Gianni Barella, the former teacher she'd wed. Teresa had also managed to obtain their phone number.

For the first time that night, Teresa called, making an excuse to slip into the kitchen.

A girl's voice answered on the other end.

After confirming it was Diana, Teresa explained. "I have your mom at my house. She's been worried sick about you. Can I get her on the phone to talk to you? I know she'll be happy to hear your voice, otherwise I wouldn't be doing this."

"Of course." Diana was delighted. "She's not angry with me though, is she?"

"I don't think so. You're her flesh and blood. I'll call her."

Teresa rested the phone down and called Nina from the dining room. "There's someone who wants to talk to you."

Nina sighed, unable to hide her exhaustion as she stood.

* * *

"Hello," Nina said, picking up the phone.

At the sound of her mother's voice, Diana started to cry. She tried to speak, but her voice was muffled.

"Whoever you are, I can't understand you."

"Mamma, Mamma, it's me. Mamma."

"Diana?" Nina burst into tears herself.

For over a minute, no words were exchanged—at least not any that could be understood. Both were sobbing and had to compose themselves before they could continue. Then, they arrived at the topic that Nina had been wanting to discuss with her daughter since the news had first reached her.

"Do you love him?"

"*Si, Mamma.*"

"Does he love you?"

"I know he does, Mamma. Not just because he says it all the time, but because of how he treats me," Diana assured her. "You're going to love him like a son. I know it."

"And what about his parents?"

"Mamma, I could never find a better mother than you, but you'll be so happy to know his parents love me. His mother is always buying me things, either for me personally or for our house. Oh, Mamma!" Diana squealed as she remembered that her mother had no idea. "they're building a house for us on his land. The architect was here the other night showing us sketches."

"*Tu sei mio gioello prezzioso, figlia mia,*" Nina said, comparing her daughter to a precious jewel. Tears shone in her eyes. "I'm not surprised that they love you. How are your grandparents?"

"They're good, Mamma. They really, really love Gianni."

"Oh is that his name?"

"Yes, Mamma, *si chiama Gianni*." Diana smiled. "And you're going to be so surprised to hear what he did! Gianni prepared all the paperwork to obtain passports for us. He wants to bring me to America so we can visit you. He knows how much you mean to me."

"*No, gioia mia,*" Nina said. She blinked the tears from her eyes. "I'm coming home this Sunday. Your sisters and I."

"Really?" Diana sounded so excited. "And Papa?"

"Your father is fine," Nina said, voice soft. "We'll talk more when I'm back."

"Mamma, I'm so happy to hear your voice, and even happier that you're coming home."

At this, the tears overflowed from Nina's eyes. She was going home to her daughter.

Yet all I've been thinking about is how difficult it will be for me to return without Nicola.

A silence fell between the phone lines. Diana broke it with a whisper. "*Perdonmi, Mamma.*"

Nina blinked the tears from her eyes. Why was her daughter apologizing?

"There's nothing to forgive," Nina said, struggling to get through her thoughts without starting to sob again. "I should have stayed in Bagheria and showed you all the love of a mother. I should never have left you. I was selfish and went searching for a love that was never there. Since I heard you eloped, I've been so worried and racked with guilt that you ran away with him because you felt neglected, because I wasn't there, because—"

"No, Mamma, no. I love Gianni."

"*Gioia mia,* I wish you only happiness in your marriage forever. That's what would make me happy again."

"I love you, Mamma."

"I love you too, *sangu mio.*" Nina took a deep breath. She couldn't believe the joy she suddenly felt at the prospect of returning. "Are you going to come to the airport to pick up your mamma?"

"Mamma, please! I'm going to sleep there the night before waiting for your arrival."

A smile spread across Nina's face.

* * *

By the time she returned to the dining room, Nina's mood was greatly improved. Her friends were overjoyed to see this.

Nina told them about her conversation with Diana and the information she'd learned about Gianni.

"I was never mad at her," Nina told them. "Who would I have been to judge? I did the same thing as a teenager. I only felt guilty because I wanted a better life for her and was afraid history was repeating itself. But Diana tells me that this Gianni is a fine man from a good family." Nina smiled. "It will be good to see her again."

"Of course," Teresa agreed.

"My daughter didn't tell me, but I'm sure she's been crying for me since I left. I know her. We all know that children are not relatives, they're much closer than that. They're part of us. Their skin, their blood, their heart and soul were made from us. They're—" Nina couldn't finish her sentence. Instead, she began sobbing once again.

Her tears put everyone in a somber mood.

"That's so true," Teresa agreed softly.

The arrival of Giacomo, Teresa's husband, broke the sad spell that had settled over the room. He came from the kitchen, carrying a large silver tray with demitasse espresso cups. In the center was a mountain of profiterole, which Teresa had baked that morning. A decadent French coffee cream coated the cream puffs, and beans had been scattered around to complete the presentation.

"Oh my, my," said Signora Anna. "This is a showcase presentation."

"And I'm sure they taste even more delicious than they look," Nina added.

* * *

After dessert, they sat around the table talking for a while longer, but they couldn't stay forever. Federal agents waited outside to ensure that Nina returned to the penthouse. Signora Anna was also watching the time.

Carlo should have already arrived, she thought. His flight had been scheduled to leave Puerto Rico earlier that same day.

"Nina, I think it's time we start saying our goodbyes," Signora Anna said. They all stood and began making their way to the door.

"Teresa, *cara mia*," Signora Anna said. "You are beautiful, warm, loving, and a generous woman. And your cooking sits right up there with your personality. Everything was delicious." She hugged Teresa, gave her a kiss, and then started to say goodbye to Giacomo.

Nina hugged Teresa next. "To say thank you for all you've done is not enough. In you, I found a sister, a friend, and the most loving person."

"Stop," Teresa said. "You're going to make me cry."

They held one another for a few minutes, both trying to hide their tears.

Their children cried openly, exchanging hugs and kisses with wet cheeks and sudden sobs.

"Mom, why do they have to go back?" Daniela asked.

"Nina has another daughter in Italy," Teresa said. "They have to go back to see her."

Chapter Thirty-Nine

Signora Anna entered the building first. George the doorman greeted her with a smile.

"Don't say anything, it a surprise," the old woman said, speaking in English so that Nina couldn't understand when she came in a few seconds after. "But is there someone upstairs?"

"*Si, Signora.*" George kept his voice soft.

Anna smiled, walking to the elevator with more pep than usual. She was excited to see her brother.

The four of them rode to the top floor.

Signora Anna fumbled for her key. Before she could find it, the door sprung open.

"It's already unlocked," Carlo said.

Nina and the kids screamed with joy. They all rushed to hug the old man. He could barely move, but a massive grin spread across his face at the response.

"*Oh Dio mio*," he said. "What a beautiful, loving welcome!" He scooped both Lilly and Gina into his arms. "Who loves these kids?"

"You do!" Both shouted.

Laughing heartily, Carlo carried them into the living room. They sat on the couch. The children didn't move from his side.

"Such a warm welcome," Signora Anna said, sitting on one of the chairs. "I'm almost jealous."

"Aww, no Signora Anna," Lilly assured her, "we love you just as much."

Carlo bounced Gina on his lap. Lilly stayed snuggled alongside him. The old man looked at Nina, and his heart ached for her. But he didn't want to ruin this happy moment.

"When you come back to New York, I want you at the house for as long as you want to stay, *hai capito*? These kids give my life meaning. My sons both live in California and I hardly see them. You, your children, and my sister are all the family I've really got."

"I really do love you, Signore Carlo."

"Enough with the Signore. From now on, call me *Papi*. That's what they say for dad in Puerto Rico. You have your father in Italy that you call *Papa*. I am under him, but not too much, eh? So you all will call me *Papi*. That is my wish."

"Okay, Papi," Nina said.

Carlo laughed. "Brava!"

As much as she didn't want to, Nina excused herself. She had to finish packing. At Carlo's request, the children stayed below with him. Nina climbed the stairs and went to the bedroom on her own.

She'd packed only a single suitcase. Even that wasn't full.

What if I can't come back?

The thought had panicked Nina before, and she'd shied away from it, assuring herself that this wouldn't be the case. Signora Anna and Signore Carlo had helped her so much and promised to continue.

Yet, despite all their generous offers, Nina didn't know how quickly she'd be able to return—or if ever. Surely, even Carlo's power had its limits.

I better pack all the girls' clothes. They won't have much back in Italy.

Nina grabbed another suitcase. She added more of her clothing and personal gifts, mixing them with her children's belongings. Soon, she reached the Gucci bag Signora Anna had gifted her.

Did she pack it? The beautiful purse wouldn't suit her life in Bagheria at all.

Diana will have more use for this than I will. She's young and newlywed.

Nina still felt uncertain about her fate. However, as she placed the Gucci bag into the suitcase, a small smile spread across her lips. Perhaps returning home wouldn't be all bad.

* * *

Friday was Nina's last day in New York.

Carlo intended to make the most of it.

After they finished with breakfast, an INS agent arrived to remove Nina's ankle monitor. Once she'd been temporarily freed, the five of them rode the elevator down. The car waited below.

Signore Carlo had planned one final, enchanting day in the city. It started with shopping. The girls purchased all the dolls and accessories they wanted, and the old man made the arrangements to have them shipped directly to Bagheria.

Next, the driver took them for ice cream at Carlo's favorite place. However, they didn't go inside and wait in line like most people. Oh no! He'd rented the entire bottom floor just for the five of them.

They took carriage rides—Carlo and the girls in one, and Nina with Signora Anna in the other. Each had a beautiful white horse pulling them. However, the one attached to Nina and Signora Anna's carriage appeared less majestic when they started to move. The poor creature pooped continuously for the trip.

Watching this from the other carriage, Signore Carlo said, "Your mamma and Signora Anna must be loving the perfume scent that their horse is giving them."

Both Lilly and Gina doubled over in laughter.

Their carriages took them to dinner at Fresco on the Green.

Before she'd even looked at the menu, Signora Anna inquired, "And will we be traveling to the ice cream shop in the same manner?"

Carlo took the cloth napkin to spread over his lap. "Of course. The carriages are ours for the evening."

"Okay, when we return, you and your two sidekicks can travel with the pooping horse."

This sent the girls into fits of laughter again.

Signora Anna, however, was serious. After a lovely dinner, when they returned to the horses, the old woman made certain to pull Nina into the other carriage with her. She wanted to punish her brother for all his jokes.

Her efforts went unrewarded.

"The horse has no more poop," Signore Carlo said to the girls as they rode toward their final destination. This joke earned him more peals of laughter.

Everyone had wanted ice cream for dessert, so their last stop was the Famous Ice Cream Shoppe. Lilly and Gina shared an outrageous banana split with lots of whipped cream. Signora Anna ordered a strawberry cheesecake sundae, and Nina got a classic warm apple pie with cold ice cream. Carlo had Nutella and banana waffles with a cup of espresso.

Their table was rich with laughter, good food, and even better company.

It filled Nina with warmth. She smiled as she ate her apple pie and looked out the window at the city beyond.

Our last night in New York, and he hasn't even attempted to see his children to say goodbye.

What a deadbeat Nick had turned out to be.

* * *

That night, after Nina and the girls had gone to bed, Carlo and Anna remained downstairs. They sat on opposite ends of the kitchen island. Each had a small glass beside them with a taste of rum that Carlo had brought with him from Puerto Rico.

Anna took a small slow sip before broaching the topic. "What will you do when they leave?"

"My next stop is Brooklyn."

"Nina doesn't want that."

Carlo downed his rum. "That bastard Niceli deserves to pay."

"Before we left this morning, I saw Lily crying behind my curtains," Anna said, sighing as she rested her glass down. "She knows more than what she lets on."

"I'm sure they both do."

"Yes, and if their father dies, they'll understand why. They're already going to have problems later with how things are going. If this happens, they'll be scared for life."

Carlo stared at his empty glass. He considered pouring another, but the urge had left him. "Why did you have to tell me all that?"

"Because I know you'll think of the girls."

"I wasn't going to kill him. He would've just had a very bad accident." Carlo's hand squeezed into a fist. "I wanted him to feel pain. He deserves—"

"Carlo, I agree a hundred percent, but we have to think of those girls, especially Lilly. She loves her father. Please, Carlo, let God take care of him."

Chapter Forty

The following day, both Signore Carlo and Signora Anna accompanied Nina and the kids to the airport.

On their way, however, Nina was allowed to stop in Dyker Heights for her final goodbyes—the most important of which was Teresa.

The minute Nina walked into the house, she went straight to her friend and wrapped her in a hug. Teresa's eyes were already red from crying.

"I'll be back soon. *Ti prego*, Teresa, *non piangere*," Nina begged her friend not to cry. "It'll kill me to think I'm leaving you in tears."

"Come on, ladies," Signora Anna said. "Let's make this a quick goodbye or it'll get worse."

With that, Teresa hugged Nina one last time. "I wish you all the happiness in the world. Have a safe trip, *mi acara amica*."

Now bawling herself, Nina said goodbye to Giacomo and hugged Daniela. Lilly and Gina did the same.

Outside, of the house more neighbors waited to say their farewells. Nina thanked them all for their kindness.

"Do you think we could also stop—just for two minutes—at Teresa's mother's home?" Nina whispered to Signora Anna. "I'll be the only who gets out to say goodbye."

"Of course."

They climbed back into the car. Lilly and Gina turned in their seats to stare out the window at Teresa and Daniela. Both stood near the sidewalk, holding one another, crying and waving.

"*Dio ti aiuta, cara mia,*" Teresa whispered, a final prayer that God would help her friend. She followed the car with her eyes until it rounded the corner.

* * *

JFK was busy as ever—cars, taxis, people departing, people arriving, people waving to hail a cab. Still, the airport's beauty remained unaffected by the traffic. JFK had a sense of orderliness, calmness, and stability. It felt like the public passing through had respect for the workers within.

Signora Anna's car stopped curbside at the Alitalia Airline pavilion. Everyone got out while the driver went to park.

"*Non pingere piu, figlia mia,*" Signora Anna said, wrapping her arms around Nina.

The old woman's request not to keep crying was impossible.

Signore Carlo carried Gina in his arms and clung to Lilly's hand as they entered the pavilion. Both girls had wet cheeks. The old man's eyes were watery as well.

Carlo had secured them first class tickets. Nina and the girls walked to the VIP desk, where the ticket agent was cordial and sweet, speaking to them in Italian without issue.

"*Buon sera, passaporti e biglietti, per favore.*"

Nina got the passport and tickets and rested them on the counter.

The agent checked through them. "Two children together with Mrs. Nina Niceli?"

"*Si.*" Nina nodded.

"No husband on this trip?" The agent asked, still trying to be cheerful and pleasant.

"*No, muriu u maritu.*"

The agent's Italian wasn't good enough to understand those words.

Signora Anna, however, smiled. She gave her brother a look, and

Carlo nodded. He understood. There was no need to kill or even hurt Nick. To Nina, her husband was already dead.

* * *

Signore Carlo and Signora Anna walked them to the gate, though the old man couldn't resist stopping at a gift shop on the way. He purchased a few things for the girls to keep them busy on the plane.

"*Ancora?*" Nina shook her head as she took the shopping bags. "You have been more than any father could be to my kids and me."

The comment almost sent the tears flowing from Carlo's eyes.

They found seats by the gate. Boarding started, but none of them were in a rush. Nina didn't stand until there were only five people left in line, and it could be avoided no longer.

"It's time for us to go," Nina said. She hugged Signora Anna close to her heart, kissing her cheeks as she thanked her. "*Grazie. Grazie di tutto.* I could never forget all that you've done for me. *Di cuore vi voglio bene.*"

I love you from the bottom of my heart as well, Signora Anna thought.

Nina then turned to Carlo, and the old man's resolve vanished. Tears pooled in his eyes. He kept biting his lower lip, trying to get rid of them. It didn't help.

Nina wrapped her arms around his neck and kissed each side of his face.

Carlo grabbed her hand and put a closed envelope into it, wrapping her fingers around it tight. "Buy all you need for you and those precious kids that I love. You don't need that bastard to send you money. I set it up so you'll receive some every month. It'll be deposited straight into your bank account."

"*No, no! No posso accettarre,*" Nina said, her initial reaction to refuse. "You've already done so much for me already."

"Of course, you can accept," Carlo argued. "Remember the deal we made? I'm your *papi*, and you're my daughter. *Ti voglio bene, figlia mia!*" He hugged and kissed the children again.

Then, they were on their way.

One daughter in her arms and the other at her side, Nina stepped forward. She took a deep breath and blinked the tears from her eyes.

Bagheria, here we come.

Nina walked straight into the tunnel toward the aircraft.

* * *

Soon, the departure area had cleared except for Carlo and Anna. They'd had to be strong for Nina and the girls. Now, however, their tears could stream openly.

"How is it possible to love someone in this magnitude in such a short time of knowing her?" Anna asked, wiping her eyes and turning to her brother.

Carlo put his arm around her shoulder. "You know what my dear sister? I'm convinced the phrase *love at first sight* isn't only for romantic love."

"I believe you're right."

Anna rested her head on her brother's shoulder. Together, they turned to the window and watched the plane. Thunder roared from its wheels as it sped forward. Soon, it lifted into the air, soaring upward.

Carlo and Anna stared until the plane carrying Nina disappeared into the clouds.

About the Author

Francesca Falletta Marceca was born in Sicily to an American-born mother and a tough Sicilian father. He was highly protective of his family and had a heart of gold. He also showed an immense amount of love to everybody in his life, a lesson that was instilled into Francesca from an early age.

She immigrated to the United States with her family when she was eight years old, adapting to a new language, food, and way of life. As her parents made significant sacrifices, she and her siblings embraced their new environment. Over the past 65 years, Francesca and her family have woven their Sicilian heritage into their American lives, never forgetting the rich culture and traditions that shaped them.

This blend of backgrounds has instilled in Francesca a deep sense of empathy and understanding—especially for those like Nina Niceli, who face the hardships of maintaining relationships amidst adversity.

Today, Francesca is a proud mother of two children who have gifted her with five adoring grandchildren. She has been happily married to her loving husband for more than 53 years. Her passions include (and will always include) writing, baking, cooking, and—most of all—giving lots of love to her family.

www.ingramcontent.com/pod-product-compliance
Lightning Source LLC
Chambersburg PA
CBHW020329170426
43200CB00006B/316